SEEING SUCCESS

SEEING SUCCESS

A Formula to Absolutely Get What
You Really, Really, **REALLY** Want!

DANNY T THOMPSON

Seeing Success

First Edition

Hardcover ISBN: 979-8-9890356-2-5
Paperback ISBN: 979-8-9890356-1-8
eBook ISBN: 979-8-9890356-0-1

CONTENTS

Introducing...

... MORE.

Do you desire more for yourself? Are you wrestling with thoughts that you should just be content with what you have and where you are? Do you avoid thinking about what your life could be because of some fear, some shame, or some story you have told yourself, and believed? Have you grown comfortable with mediocrity? Or are you just stuck? Do you feel as if you are going nowhere, and you just don't know how to get moving toward the life you have always wanted?

If you answered *yes* to any of these questions, this book is for you. And even if things are going pretty well for you, could you be happy with more?

In this book, you will find a formula for how you CAN absolutely get what you really, really, *really* want! You may scoff, shake your head, or draw horns on my photo on the back flap–but it is true. I personally absolutely guarantee that when you follow the formula, you will be on your way to having what you really want, and eventually, having it all.

Let me ask this question: Are you currently living up to your potential? I have yet to hear anyone answer *yes* to this question with absolute conviction. Think about it: Can we truly know our potential? As far as I know, the only way to even begin to know our full potential is to keep pressing, to keep on moving forward toward MORE. In fact, I built my coaching company, I Am More Performance Coaching, on this truth.

Go ahead. Say it: *I am more.* How does that feel? Now say it like you mean it. Say it again.

If you allow yourself to be honest, then you know, deep inside, this is the truest statement you can make: *I am more than who I am right now, and I am capable of growth and learning.*

I have seen, and have been observing, that the vast majority of humans are living *less-than* lives. Many of us just aren't really showing up as our best **self** most of the time. That is not intended to be an insult. I am including myself in that statement. I am also including the most successful person I know, as well as the wide-eyed newbie walking through the door at any one of my training events. Each of us has potential that remains untapped, and if we are willing to look deep inside, there is almost always a yearning to do more…to be more. Here is the good news: When we do take a step forward, and we begin to tap into that potential, we gain knowledge and skills, and we grow. And as we grow, we open ourselves to even more potential, even more possibilities. Get comfortable with this idea: No matter how much success you have seen, or how many struggles you have overcome, there is more to you–more to have, more to do, more to be. In some ways, this can be scary, but really, believing and internalizing this is the beginning of freedom. We do not have to remain who we are right now. In fact, we shouldn't. We are more. Our past has no hold over us, and our current abilities and knowledge do not trap us. We are more than who we are right now.

LOOKING IN THE MIRROR

I look in the mirror and I know, deep inside, I am more than the person looking back at me is in that moment. I can be more than who I am right now. What about you? What do you see when you look at your reflection? No matter where you currently are in your career, business, or life, if you are willing to be truthful to yourself, you know that you are *definitely* more. Are you okay with that truth? Now, are you willing to do something about it? This book is about uncovering the MORE that you really are!

Here is one thing I have witnessed, as a coach, and as an observer of humans: Relatively few are truly successful. And when you consider the number of people in the world, even fewer, as a percentage, are *wildly* successful. Why is that? I have heard many ideas about why people live mediocre lives or settle for less. Some attribute it to lack of opportunity, racial discrimination, physical handicaps, socio-economic barriers, or even geography. While I will concede there are many valid obstacles along the road to success, you will have to agree with me that there are at least a few examples of wildly successful people who have faced those obstacles mentioned above, as well as many, many others, and yet, somehow, they achieved amazing things! We hear the stories all the time; in fact, often these overcomers are brought to the stage to tell us how they did it. We drink in their story, we cheer and clap, and we leave the show inspired with new intentions of doing something big. And after a while that buzz fades and we slowly fall back into mediocrity–living our *less-than* lives.

If going to an event and seeing someone who has achieved greatness in some form would launch us into our own success, this formula I am presenting wouldn't be needed. But motivational speakers and their events only take you so far, and to BE more, you need more than a moment of inspiration. The Seeing Success formula is not a pep talk or a get-rich scheme. It is a proven formula that absolutely will help you get what you want, and this book includes tools, tactics, and strategies to help you stay motivated and focused so that you can keep moving forward into the More that you are.

I contend that if one person can achieve great things, anyone and everyone can achieve great things. It isn't about giftedness or special abilities, which, granted, some people do possess–and that certainly doesn't hurt. But really, it is about time on task. It's about doing the right activities at the right time, and more often than not, doing them repeatedly. Has someone experienced wild success in the field or career that you would like to pursue? That means it can be done. There is absolutely no reason why you shouldn't–or can't–have the life you have always wanted…and even more. So, yes, you can have what you really, really, *really* want. My question now is this: Do you even ***know*** what you really want?

I believe, bottom line, the difference between those who achieve greatness and those who do not is this simple truth: Those who have achieved have had a powerful sense of what they wanted and a willingness to do the work. That's it. Despite all barriers and obstacles you may face, if you are willing to do the hard work of digging deep to identify that "thing" you really, really, *really* want, you will begin to see that success. And when you commit to doing the right activities daily to pursue what you really want, you will see more success. Keep it up and you will *have* your success, whatever that looks like to you.

WHAT DO YOU WANT?

If you are still reading, then I suspect there is a voice in your head asking, "What DO I really want?" Sadly, it may be an unfamiliar voice. Chances are you haven't thought about it much lately. I mean, life is busy. I get it. There are demands on our time all day long. We go to work, the phone keeps ringing, the emails keep coming in, the texts, the tweets, the posts, and chats. Then we go home and there is the yard, the laundry, the cleaning, the bills–stuff just keeps coming. We watch a bit of TV and fall asleep exhausted, only to rise and do it again. Often, we can get caught up in the repetition, put it on autopilot, and forget that at one time we really wanted more than this. It's human nature to adapt to what is, and forget about the what-can-be. We get used to things as they are and sometimes just stop wondering, "Could things be different? Is this what I really want?"

I know a woman who has told me in no uncertain terms, "I don't want anything." This breaks my heart because I know that is a lie she has come to believe over time. I know the details of her past fairly well, and this little 4-foot-11-inch dynamo has faced some pretty difficult times–more than some, less than others. What I see that she doesn't see is that she has faced them, and beaten the odds. She has remained faithful to her husband through challenging times, kept a beautiful home for many years, and raised a brilliant and successful son. She is one of the top designers in her city, and now is a partner in a business that leverages her particular talent. Frankly, I am impressed, and yet, somehow, she is not. Something is wrong with her current perspective, as she does not see in herself what others see, and so she says she doesn't want anything. Rather than desiring more, she has chosen to adopt the label for herself: *I am a realist.* This statement has become her personal mantra and a way to help her accept things as they are. But it's a cop-out, in my opinion. As I see it, choosing to see limitations as *That's just the way it is*, and identifying as a realist are just ways to avoid venturing out into the unknown. She is playing the victim and choosing to navigate her life by keeping her head down and just letting life happen to her, come-what-may. She sees the negative in almost every opportunity, which keeps her from reaching for more. Her glass remains half empty, at best.

But it doesn't have to be that way. With the right perspective, she could have anything she wanted, and her current success would just be the starting point. What if being realistic, rather than seeing the negative side, is actually recognizing that we really can have what we really, really, *really* want? If she were willing, and would lift up her head, look around, and see what I see, she just might start to dream about ***more***. She just might start seeing ***more*** for herself. She would start seeing success.

STUCKNESS

If you are a young person, maybe in college or just out of school, and not into the "rat race" yet, you may be one of the many who find themselves stuck. When I worked for Gary Keller, co-founder and Chairman of the Board at Keller Williams Realty International, I was blessed to lead an effort to create a national nonprofit organization focused on overcoming this epidemic of "stuckness" raging among young adults. This put me in a position to talk to many teachers, trainers, and curriculum developers, as well as thousands of young adults facing the big decision of what to do with their lives. Without exception, all agreed that most schools today do not challenge students to think about changing the world or pursuing their dreams. At least here in the United States, most of our schools are focused on passing tests. By focusing on test scores, they train our youth to think there is always a right answer and a wrong answer, so you just need to have the answers. The curriculum is designed to give them that answer, which they are instructed to memorize. And, when and if they ever do talk about the future, they are often given aptitude tests, told what career would suit them best, and encouraged to go to college to learn some more answers.

Essentially, much of traditional schooling trains our young people to decide on a career when they are 17, choose a college, graduate, get a job, and work it until they retire. And here is the problem: that isn't the world we live in anymore. While recently in the United States, we have the lowest unemployment rate in the history of our country, most people change jobs an average of every five years. And often, it is a career change, sometimes out of necessity, sometimes out of boredom or dissatisfaction. Life is moving at such a fast pace. Technology changes daily, and some jobs disappear, while new skills and knowledge are requirements for keeping a good job, and even more so for advancement. Memorizing the answers does not work in this economy. And if you are 17, or 20, how in the hell are you supposed to decide what the rest of your life is supposed to look like? That can be frightening. No wonder so many are stuck.

That said, being stuck isn't reserved for the 17-year-old. Many adults in the workforce find themselves in a career that sounded good on paper, and yet they feel no sense of satisfaction. The passion is gone, and it feels like there is no purpose. What seemed like a good fit, simply, is not. Let the rat-race commence.

THERE IS A BETTER WAY

A growing number of leaders in the education industry have identified this issue as well and are doing something about it. Programs are being designed and have been implemented that do not focus on memorizing the answers; rather, space is allowed so that the questions originate from the students. The questions AND the answers are generated by the students having conversations with each other, with the teacher acting as more of a facilitator. No answers are provided. They are being taught to think, to ask, to investigate, to mastermind with others. And when students arrive at answers, they are encouraged to test them out. As they test answers, students gather and examine information, and then formulate new questions and answers that are then tested and examined, and so on. Armed with this skill, students going through such programs are far better prepared for the world of possibilities. Hopefully, this becomes a trend and excellence becomes the norm. One can always hope.

In the same way, the Seeing Success formula challenges you to ask great questions and to be willing to investigate, to examine the evidence and results, and to mastermind with others. It is imperative that we stay curious and open minded, be willing to ask tough questions, and face the answers with courage and honesty. You must admit that when you know the truth of the situation, you are far more likely to act appropriately and make better choices in that situation. This is true in life, and this is true in business. The better way, if you aren't doing this already, is to *challenge* your beliefs. Be certain that what you believe is true. Since Truth can withstand all scrutiny, you will either grow in your understanding of your beliefs, or you will discover you are wrong. Either way, it is good for you. Ignorance is *not* bliss.

I know what I know, and it's possible I am wrong, and so I am working to learn more each day.

THE BEST QUESTION

Keeping all of that in mind, I believe that the most important question—the first question—you must ask is this: What do I really, really, *really* want? Ask often. Answer to the best of your ability each time. Test. Investigate. Examine. Mastermind. When you do, you will change the world. At the very least, you will change YOUR world.

So, I am asking: What do you want? I mean really, really, *really* want?

You picked up this book for some reason. Let's be honest–what we really want is rarely just more money, though that is certainly acceptable (and frankly, helpful). If we take the time to really think about it, what we really, really, *really* want is directly connected to WHO we really want to be, with how we see ourselves in the future. No matter how we articulate it, ultimately as we aim at more of something, we end up becoming more ourselves. Which again opens us up to even more. And the cycle continues. It is my perspective that our full potential is only truly reached when we leave this world and enter the next one. Then, upon entering Eternity, we will be complete. I believe that is our destiny. We are supposed to experience success. We are created to have what we really, really, *really* want.

Let me clarify something right here: I am a follower of Jesus Christ, so my worldview is that this world is not all there is. I am not asking you to agree with me if you believe differently. You don't have to have this same perspective to benefit from this book. I simply believe it is important to be candid about how I view the world to help you see what I see. Our worldview shapes how we see everything else (hence the phrase "worldview").

A LITTLE BIT ABOUT ABUNDANCE

There is a Scripture that says that "we are more than conquerors," and another that says God intends us to experience an abundant life.[1] From these words, and the whole of Scripture, which I personally consider to be thoughts directly from the Creator of the universe, I understand that I am created to enjoy the abundance of life. I understand that I am designed to be a winner, and to conquer the obstacles I come up against on my journey to abundance. I interpret this–and have experienced personally–that the universe is for me, not against me. My destiny is not failure, but success! Abundance, not mediocrity!

1 The Scripture on conquerors is found in Romans 8:37, and John 10:10 refers to the "[life] to the full" that God intends for His people (New International Version).

I am to have purpose and meaning, not just get through the day. I am destined to pursue and achieve the longings of my heart. Therefore, when I do encounter challenges and what may appear to those on the outside looking in as failures, those challenges and obstacles are only lessons I need to learn. They help me grow the skills and the mental muscles I need to keep moving forward. I am challenged to think and deliberate, to ask good questions, and to figure out how to overcome, since I am, in fact, an overcomer. And I have news for you: so are you!

If your worldview differs from mine, again, no judgment. This is not an evangelical book. I only needed to share my core perspective with you to give you a deeper understanding of why I believe we were designed for more. Clarity is important at all times, so I needed to be clear about this. I will also state that I realize I am far from perfect. I cuss (even in this book), I drink alcohol, I occasionally smoke, as well as other foolish things. So if you are a follower of Jesus, and you are expecting this book to be filled with Scripture and for me to exude Christlikeness, you may be disappointed. I can be an a-hole sometimes (just ask my wife). It would be a good idea to get over it. Let's just stay on point and work on getting you what you really, really, *really* want.

So, in the pursuit of clarity, here is what this formula isn't:

It isn't something magical, or mystical, or something recently discovered during a spirit walk or a vision quest. In fact, the core of the formula is old, common, and even to some degree, well-known already. It exists in many forms and has been taught for many years. What is new is the way this formula is being presented based on years of coaching, leading businesses and employees, and failing, and failing–and succeeding.

Also, this isn't easy, nor is it a get-rich-quick scheme. As simple as the four steps may look, if it were easy, more people would be wildly successful. Far and wide, men and women who "know" some form of this formula continue to struggle, stumble, and live without the things they really want. I have witnessed this over and over, and this book is my attempt at providing more clarity about what is important in the steps; where you must lean in, dig deep, and press hard; as well as the specific tactics, habits, and actions that make the difference between success and less-than-success.

With that being said, let's move on to what this book is:

The first part deals directly with what goes on in between the ears: our thoughts. That's a biggie, and many books have been written just on that singular topic. I do recommend many other writers on this and have read much of what is out there. I have been studying behavior and mindset for literally 30 years, so I hope to offer enough in that area to give you an understanding that you can–and must–take control of your thoughts. More on that later. Keep reading. The rest of the book is tactical, complete with forms and systems to follow specifically.

This book is also about success in any area of life you want to improve. It is crafted specifically for the business owner and anyone wanting to grow their business, but the formula can be used for quite literally anything you want to achieve. I have used it to learn to play guitar, to become more empathetic, to grow my coaching skills, and to complete remodeling projects on homes I have purchased over the years. You can use it to overcome bad habits, to instill good ones, to become a better parent and spouse–pretty much anything you can imagine. The formula is used essentially the same way, regardless of the goal. If you want more in any area of your life, keep reading.

In some ways, this book is a partial story of my life. I have been told by some after having read my bio that it appears to have been an interesting life. All I can say is I have been blessed to have been able to do a LOT of different things, and each of those opportunities has added perspective to craft and fine-tune this formula. Each experience has in some way added to my process in pursuing success. As careers go, I have been a carpenter, electrician, remodeling contractor, house flipper, investor, realtor, pastor, publisher, corporate executive, nonprofit executive, educator, business coach, insurance agency owner, property manager, and ranch owner. I still own multiple properties as well as interest in a few businesses. I am an author and a coach, a teacher and a consultant. All these opportunities have put me in the position of constantly having to research, learn new things, and venture into the unknown. I have seen success in each opportunity by leveraging some form of the Seeing Success formula. And, by the way, I have had–and am having–a hell of a lot of fun.

I have also been blessed to work with some very amazing people, some of the very best in their fields. I hesitate to start naming them only because there have been so many influential, inspirational, and wildly successful men and women in my life that I would likely skip over one or two. Or ten. As a publisher, I recall sitting around a table with the team doing our best to name every person who contributed to the project to include in the acknowledgements…and still missing someone.

In this book I have woven in stories of some of those people and experiences, when appropriate, to bring home a point or illuminate an idea. When credit needed to be given to someone, I provided their name. Throughout this book, I share specific stories about my experiences with my coaching clients to illuminate a truth or struggle. Instead of using their real names, I am using some form or the name "Robert." (In part to hide their identities, but mainly because I found it amusing.) The stories are all true: I am only changing the names for privacy's sake. So–let's get to it.

PART I
First Things First

This book in your hands is a handbook and a workbook, as well as a textbook, on how to get what you really, really, *really* want. For some of you, reading it once may be enough to get you launched and headed toward massive success. But if you are anything like me, you may need to read it a few times and keep it handy to go back and dig into a blind spot, a pothole on the road to success. Along the journey to your success, I guarantee there will be bumps, roadblocks, and potholes. Often, a pothole is something you could not have foreseen, whether a natural manifestation of a mountain to overcome, or a roadblock put up by someone to slow you down, whether intentional or not. Sometimes, if you are watching carefully, you can see these roadblocks ahead of time and avoid them completely. The point here is that falling into a hole is sometimes your fault for one reason or another, and other times simply unavoidable. Knowing more about the terrain in advance can help you get around the potholes with minimal bumps and bruises, help you stay alert, and speed things up on the road to success. The bottom line is that getting what you really, really, *really* want, will involve challenges, and even failures, along the way. I am providing some tools to help you avoid as many of these as possible as well as providing guidance on how to get out of the hole once you are in it. The big issue here is that potholes are simply a part of the journey. When you hit one, I'll give you five minutes to bitch and moan about it, then encourage you to get up and get on with it.

THE ANALOGY

Here I want to present an analogy that I will refer to often as we move through the steps in the following chapters. I have already mentioned potholes and other references to being on a journey. Let's liken the Success Journey to a car trip across the country: Just as we can select a wonderful and exciting destination for a road trip, we can choose whatever we want for the destination of our lives. We can go someplace special and scenic, or we can spin our wheels and stay where we are. We can pursue our destiny, or we can put the vehicle in park and just hang out. The glue to this analogy is that we are all on a journey from our birth to our death. We are going somewhere, and it is up to us whether we choose to direct ourselves to a particular destination or go with the flow, or even just stay put. By now you have noticed I believe without reservation that we have tremendous control over our destination. Many very capable, awesome, wonderful people do not have *their* success simply because they have not chosen to get intentional; in terms of the analogy, a destination has not been chosen. You may be one of those capable, awesome, wonderful people. I believe what is provided in this book can change all that. I will be leveraging this journey analogy often and will build on it as we progress. I encourage you to come with me on this journey.

At the beginning of each step, after introducing the concept, I open with **The Route**. This is the specific method or process of how to successfully execute that particular step. Clarity is key; you need to get a crystal-clear understanding of the step and how to make sure you execute it correctly and fully. While there is definitely some flexibility in the process, the biggest potholes, as I have seen over and over, are the "shortcuts." I love riding mountain bikes, and in the hills of Austin, Texas, there are amazing trails everywhere. When I first began discovering the trails, often, when it was time to go home, I would look for a shortcut to get back to my truck. Far too often, the shortcut was not a shortcut at all. Numerous times, arriving home hours late, I would have to explain to my wife how I had gotten lost. She would give me that look–if you are married, you know the look I am talking about. If I had a map of that trail, I would have returned on time and not had to endure the "look" at all. And of course, years later, having ridden those trails many times, I was able to navigate my time, as well as my results. The Seeing Success formula is a map to your success. Until you know your way around, stick to the route.

When appropriate, a section entitled **The Toolbox** is included to provide some tools that are helpful in the implementation of the step. **The Potholes** section is to identify common obstacles you may face on this journey. Each chapter ends with **The Potential** to help you get extremely clear about what is at stake: *your success*! When you know what to do, how to do it, what to watch out for, and *why* you are doing it, you can stay focused and empowered to do what must be done. You can have what you really, really, *REALLY* want.

GETTING CLEAR

The struggles I have experienced as well as observed in watching others have been primarily due to lack of clarity: clarity about what the goal looks like when it is reached, clarity about the path to the results desired, and clarity about what specifically needs to be done each day to achieve the sub-goals along the way. The power of the Seeing Success formula is that it is all about how to get clarity and how to stay clear about what you really want.

One of the unique things about our coaching program at I Am More Performance Coaching is that we incorporate the DISC behavior profiles in every conversation. I recognize many organizations use some type of behavior assessment at the time of hiring new team members, and that is awesome. I do too. We continue that conversation with our employees and our clients and teach them to understand their own behavior as well as leverage the behavior profiles to be able to succeed with others. The Golden Rule is to "Treat others the way you want to be treated." The Platinum Rule is to "Treat others the way THEY want to be treated." The DISC system is a great tool to improve communication skills as well as know yourself better. In this book, I have incorporated this tool as well. If you are unfamiliar with the DISC profiles, google it or visit my coaching website for more info. It's a fascinating topic.

THE BIGGEST OBSTACLE

Let me also say from the onset that your biggest obstacle will be you. You have no doubt heard the expression, *You are your own worst enemy.* Yeah, we have all been there. The expression is true only because we only know what we know, and we don't know what we don't know. Therefore, when you set a goal on something you have never done before, you must base it on what you currently know combined with your best guess. As you pursue the goal, you will run into things you have not experienced before. Resistance (aka, fear) can kick in, and the mind can start finding reasons why you should stop and stick to what you know. For most humans, our default address is the Comfort Zone. Playing it "safe." Thought habits take over because it is easier to keep doing what we have been doing. We are far too often happy enough in our own little world of familiarity, and so our thoughts work to find ways to justify staying put. There are two problems with this line of thought:

1. The things outside of your comfort zone that you are afraid of are also inside your comfort zone (e.g., failure, sickness, potholes, etc.).
2. What you really, really, really want is NOT located in your comfort zone.

You can't get there by standing still. You must move. If you *want* something different, you must *do* something different. You must venture into the unknown. The good news is that you don't have to go in blind. The Seeing Success formula provides a framework to navigate your life toward what you really, really, *really* want. I promise.

THINKING ABOUT THOUGHTS

Have you ever had someone ask you why you acted a certain way and you replied, "I don't know"? Perhaps you have heard someone state that they did something "without thinking." Here's the thing: even when we think we acted without thinking, we did think. Even if we struggle to identify the specific thoughts that caused us to act, or react, in a certain way, there are thoughts in our mind that took us there. You may have heard this referred to as "our programming." A series of thoughts occurs, or a program executes, and then you act. Much like a computer program, written in specific code, all actions, like it or not, are a result of thought, or a series of thoughts. I prefer to call the series of thoughts ***thought habits.*** I define a thought habit as *a mental process we develop over time which results in executing quickly without deep examination.*

From the moment we were born, we have been developing thought habits which help us speed up each new process we learn**.** A baby cries. Daddy comes and picks her up. The child learns that Daddy is good and crying brings comfort. She learns crying gets her what she wants. Data gathered. The baby attempts to walk. The brain begins to assess which muscles to move, how to balance, and what to expect. The baby falls. Momma catches the baby. The baby just learned that Momma is safe and it's okay to keep trying. Data gathered. A toddler screams "No!" and either gets what he wants or gets put into time-out. Data gathered. And so it goes our entire life. Based on the information we gather, thought habits are being created and entrenched. Our brain is literally wiring itself for efficiency. When we see something new, or do something new, we must think more slowly and contemplate to understand it and fit it into our perspective.[2] But our minds do not necessarily want to waste all that time thinking deeply. The most basic truth about the human body is that it was designed to preserve itself and conserve its resources. Our brain is always working to be efficient,

2 Some of my ideas about the mind and how we think come from Daniel Kahneman's 2011 best seller, *Thinking Fast and Slow*.

and it does so by networking the neural pathways to speed up thought processes. It works to get from thought to action as fast as possible, and so it "looks" for patterns and shortcuts, and "wires" itself accordingly. As a result, due to the data we have gathered along the way, we habitually think through things in ways that have been successful for us before. We literally create pathways in our mind that make certain thought processes go much, much faster. So fast, we sometimes appear to act without thought. But rest assured: we did think.

PURPOSEFUL ENGAGEMENT[3]

You likely have heard someone refer to muscle memory as it relates to playing an instrument or a sport. When I was 38, I decided I was going to learn how to play guitar. My sister, who is an amazing musical talent, lent me her guitar. I made a schedule, and committed to practicing an hour a day, five days a week, with the goal of being able to play at a youth camp that was in six months. At that time, I was a full-time pastor and during the week there were few people around. I scheduled lunch time alone in a quiet room, bought a book on learning guitar, and began the torturous process. At first, I had to intentionally think about every placement of every finger. With intense purpose, focusing on the left hand, then the right. Day by day, week by week, month by month. At first, I didn't see any improvement, or so I thought. My fingertips hurt and developed callouses. I kept going although I could barely stand the sound of that guitar. One day, about three months in, I played a full song, beginning to end, without error. Elated, I was energized and stayed with it. I continued to practice, and more and more, time on task, my fingers landed on the right strings and the guitar made more beautiful sounds. Practice makes excellence. I hit my goal and led worship at that youth camp. I continued to

3 This term is from Robert Sternberg's assertion that the IQ test is too narrow and doesn't take into account creativity as part of intelligence. He wrote that the major factor in whether people achieve expertise "is not some fixed prior ability, but purposeful engagement." Robert Sternberg is Professor of Human Development at Cornell University, and is a major contributor to psychology in the 20th century.

practice and improve and went on to become one of the worship leaders at my home church for over ten years.

Here's the deal: the muscles in my fingers do not actually have a memory. My brain gathered data and began to make connections to speed up the thoughts behind each finger movement. The more I practiced with purposeful engagement, the more it created connections and wired itself to streamline the many small thoughts that were occurring separately into a series of thoughts occurring quickly. Reading, setting my fingers, moving my hands, and all the thoughts connecting all of it into a flow. Remember, the brain wants efficiency at all costs. So then, the thought habits developed over time and with intention have enabled me to now grab a guitar and play a song I just heard, and even sing while playing the notes and chords. From hearing to playing, the path has been wired efficiently over time with repetition with my intention to improve my playing. In addition, the more I learn about music theory and the relationship of the chords and notes, the more capable I am of determining the chord progression and altering and changing the finger patterns of my left and right hand simultaneously. It may appear to be without thought, but it in fact requires much thought: thought habits wired with precision over time so that the process becomes seamless and almost instantaneous. The key thoughts are still happening, just much, much faster because the pathways have been created, removing contemplation moments, and streamlining the process.

IT TAKES TIME

So, you see, if you want to master a musical instrument, you will absolutely need to purposefully engage your mind to create specific thought habits over time through repetition. Similarly, if you want to leverage sales scripts and master the closing of a sale, this too, is time on task. Bringing this into the Seeing Success conversation: The first time we think of something we know nothing about, we rely on what we do know to attempt to understand it. Literally, our brains search for any information we already know to relate it to this thing we do not know. We interpret this thing best we can, then make a choice, or a conclusion, and we act, or choose not to act. Based on outcomes, very quickly, we develop new thought habits that we then leverage to decide more quickly. That is why analogies are effective for learning. We need a "this is like that" to help us navigate the unknown. Every new thing we learn associates itself with something we already know. We may use the phrase, "That blows my mind!" when we see or hear something that we simply cannot immediately find a match for in our memories, so we have to slow down our thoughts to figure it out. The brain is always looking for a shortcut, and if an activity or situation is repeated, a new pathway is created, and, if it is important to us, a new thought habit is born. Understanding this natural process going on in our minds unleashes the capacity to be intentional about what we learn and who we choose to become. Recognizing it takes time on task to gain the knowledge and skills you need for your success confirms that who you are and what you can do today are just the beginning. There is more. You are more. And tomorrow, you will be even more.

GAINFULLY AWARE

Awareness is the key to choosing well. It may sound obvious, but far too often, we act a certain way simply because it is how we have always acted. Habits are powerful, intentional or not. I highly recommend *The Power of Habit* by Charles Duhigg to dig more deeply into this science, but for now, suffice it to say that we must choose to become aware of the actions we choose and why we choose them, and then choose the very best in alignment with our Success Vision. There's a whole lotta choosing going on. Make sure you are choosing well.

It is also important to be aware that when we are focused on some type of work requiring us to process, consider, and make many decisions, our brains use large amounts of energy. That is why we come home exhausted even though we may have spent all day behind a computer screen sitting in a chair. Will power is often weaker at night, after a long day. Our brains get tired, and when that happens, the brain takes the easy path, the thought habit that is already entrenched. If you have a habit of eating ice cream at night and you are attempting to change that habit to be healthier or lose weight, to resist that thought habit requires intention and energy. When you are tired, somehow that bowl of ice cream ends up empty on your nightstand…again.

We need to be aware that our brain is always creating thought habits, rewiring for greater efficiency and for conservation of energy. Whether we are aware or not, it is leveraging every bit of data it has available. The data that is most available (top of mind) is leveraged first, and if that doesn't work, we go into contemplation mode. The brain literally searches for more data that may not be connected directly to any current thought habit. The good news is that we do not need to be slaves to our minds, and we can choose to leverage this searching mechanism to get what we want and become more efficient. We can be more purposeful about developing the thought habits that empower us and drive us down the road to our success. We can also identify those thoughts that do not serve us, or even hinder us, on our journey to what we really want, and replace those thought habits with better ones.

Understanding how your mind works and leveraging a process to harness the right thought habits about the right actions and activities, as well as replacing those thought habits that are hurting you, will propel you toward having the life you really want.

THOUGHTS MAKE YOU OR BREAK YOU

Let's explore this idea about thoughts and habits a bit more because it is a core issue in the pursuit of getting what you really want. Your thoughts will make you or break you. If you are subject to thoughts that lead you to decisions you later regret, which include action and inaction, then it will take much longer to achieve your success. In fact, since your thoughts cause you to act in the world, your *being* is the net result of your thoughts. If that is true, it then stands to reason that we should harness our thoughts to become who we want to be, and act how we prefer to act so we can get what we want to get.

Look at it this way: if I have thought habits that are not moving me toward my goals, then they are getting in my way, slowing me down. If I choose better thoughts and harness thought habits to yield better results, I will get what I want sooner and with fewer potholes and detours.

Have you ever jumped to a conclusion only to find later you were absolutely wrong? Has anyone ever done that to you? Yeah–not so fun. I can think of many examples, but I don't want to throw anyone (or myself) under the bus. Let's just admit it now: We all do this. Something happens, thought habit occurs, and we draw a conclusion without contemplation. Boom! We have now caused a problem. Based on our past experiences, we make decisions quickly. The potential for being wrong is always there, especially in a new situation (and especially if you are married). The mind is lazy, and it always searches for patterns from our past to understand the current moment we are in, and if we aren't careful, we can blow it. Adding to that, because our minds are searching *quickly* for something to align and fit for efficiency's sake, we literally overlook things. The key here, again, is awareness.

Understanding how thought habits reign in our minds, helping us and hindering us, it's clear that scheduling time for contemplation is the pathway to success. I am so serious right now. You must schedule *thinking* time. I have known many highly successful people who have great demands on their time, and who get a lot done in one day. And all of them, literally every single one of them, have specific time in their day to slow down and think. During that time, you can review the results of your recent actions and look for anything that isn't working or isn't getting you the results you intended. You can look for any thoughts that might be causing you to overlook something. You can think about upcoming activities and contemplate a deeper view. You can question some of your conclusions, just to make sure you aren't jumping to any of them.

I know you may be thinking, *I am so busy; how can I possibly take any time out of my day just to contemplate?* I absolutely promise you that one hour (or more) spent thinking will help you identify potential time wasters, find better solutions to current issues, and bring you a peace that is indescribable. The truth is, left to themselves, our minds are lazy and always looking for shortcuts. Conversely, our minds are powerful and capable of so much creativity that given the time to slow down and contemplate, almost anything is possible. We must learn to practice awareness, identify thought habits–good and bad–and slow down regularly.

TELL A BETTER STORY

Here is another truth for you: YOU are responsible for your thoughts. When you have thoughts that cause you grief, deter you from your right efforts, or lead you to react to something poorly, that is on you. I have heard more than one person defend their bad behavior by claiming, "Well, that is just the way I am." Yeah…BULL! That is the same as quitting. Or how about this one: "They made me angry." Really? They **made** you? No one can ***make*** you anything, unless they put a gun to your head. Here is what is really going on: Someone does something, and, in a split-second, you think about that something, and you choose a meaning to associate with that something based on your thought habits, create a story about what is happening, which you blindly believe, and then act. If you choose anger, some story you have written and believed has led you to that emotion. If you choose compassion, that too is from a story you believe, from thought habits that led you to that emotion. Both anger and compassion, then, can be responses to that thing someone did. Your reaction to something always comes from the meaning you give to that something.

We are all storytellers. And the stories we tell ourselves are directly connected to our thought habits. When we tell ourselves the story, "That person is trying to make me angry" or "That person is disrespecting me," can we really be so sure? Even if we know them well, do we really know the true intention of the act that we are assigning meaning to? It is possible they had no intention at all of making you mad. It is possible they are telling themselves a story about you that is as off-base as the one you have told yourself. We act from what we believe. And we believe our own stories.

By becoming more aware of the stories we tell ourselves, we can shape our reactions to serve us better and get what we really want. By choosing a better story, we can direct our responses to be more in alignment with our Success Journey and remove some of the potholes.

I am going to share with you a powerful phrase that has kept me free from potential regret many times over. Many people I have shared this with have later told me this phrase has given them freedom as well. Start each story you tell yourself about another person with this phrase: *They are doing the best they can with what they know.* This simple truth, stated in your mind every time you encounter someone causing turbulence in your life, will change everything once you truly believe it. Mark Willis, former CEO of Keller Williams Realty International, taught me this concept. His contagious smile, optimistic energy, and intentional hope enters the room minutes before he does, and he believes the very best of each person he meets. Because of him, I do too. And, upon believing that everyone is really trying their best, it freed me from many unnecessary burdens. I don't have to forgive, because I am no longer offended. It has removed many roadblocks in my life.

Seriously. Try it: think of someone who is irritating you or causing you grief in some way. Do you have them in your mind? Now say it: *They are doing the best they can with what they know.* Say it again. Choose to believe it. When that statement is true to you, whatever it is you are holding against them isn't their fault. They aren't doing anything to you on purpose. They are simply doing the best they can with what they currently know. The challenge then is to decide, *How can I help them to know better?*

Let's take this a step further: Whoever hurt you in the past, forgive them. They were doing the best they could with what they knew at the time, and more than likely, it wasn't about you anyway. And even if it was, seriously, why give them power over your life? There is no reason to allow their stuff to be your stuff. Let it go. Let *them* go.

You see? How does that feel? You are no longer angry or upset at them, but rather looking for an opportunity to help them. That story you have told yourself about them changes how you respond to them. It changes you. Think about the kind of person that makes you, and how you then begin to contribute to their growth, instead of just being angry. You no longer waste energy on unprofitable emotions, but you bring contribution to them, and to your world. That energy empowers you, and people notice and are attracted to you because of it. And here is the kicker: since you don't know their real intention anyway, why not choose a better story that ends up creating an opportunity to help them on their journey, and even possibly, ends up helping you as well?

MIND YOUR MIND

Try this statement: *This is the way I am now,* ***and*** *I am learning every day, becoming more.* THAT is a powerful statement, and it is always true, provided you are willing to take responsibility for your thoughts. I want to challenge you to "mind your mind." What I mean is that we must pay attention to our thoughts and examine what those thoughts lead us to do. I was riding the Tube in London and noticed the sign above the doors: "Mind the Gap." If you haven't ridden commuter trains before, there is a small gap between the train and the platform. As you can imagine, a slight misstep could result in a fall and, depending on the number of commuters, serious injury. So when the doors open, people exit and enter and are reminded every time to pay attention to the gap. While many people in Europe leverage these trains multiple times each day, they still need to be reminded of the gap. It seems we get so used to some things that we eventually don't even see them, which could end badly. You and I, we need to mind our mind. We must pay attention to our thoughts and where they take us, lest we stumble and fall. We are responsible for our every thought.

I have had pushback on this idea. Some insist they cannot control their every thought. In the Scripture there is a verse that says, "Take every thought captive." (2 Corinthians 10:5 technically says take every thought captive for Christ, but that is another discussion for another time.) We are admonished to take captive the thoughts we have and direct them to become our better selves. I believe that because it says we can, we can in fact take any and every thought captive. Therefore, we are responsible for our thoughts. If you are struggling with this idea, I need you to trust me and just choose to believe it. Once you take responsibility for your thoughts, you can then do something about them. Awareness and accountability lead to change and growth. Our thought habits can take us down the path of failure or success. We get to choose. We must choose well.

Let's go a little deeper. I want you to think about a time you snapped at someone angrily. If you are married or have a long-time relationship, I am willing to bet you have reacted inappropriately to something your partner said at least once or twice. I have been married for 38 years and on more than one occasion, I immediately regretted the words that came out of my mouth. (I know you are saying now, *No, Danny T. That can't be! You are a Christian!* Yep. And I also warned you I can be an a-hole as well.) Think about that reaction and the words you blurted out and consider what you were thinking in that moment. What thoughts caused you to react in that way?

In my case, at least relating to a poor reaction recently, my wife said something that made me feel disrespected. I told myself a story about her disrespect. Thoughts led to feelings, feelings to action. The resulting action was immediately regretted. So, where did that feeling come from? What thought habit specifically led me there to that point of regret? Where did that story come from? When I took time to mind my mind (later in this case, unfortunately), and take those thoughts captive, I was able to see she was not being disrespectful at all, but that I have a fear of her disrespecting me. The truth is that I care about what she thinks of me so much that it hurts me when I believe she is disappointed in me. Because of that underlying fear, I told a story that assigned meaning to her words, meaning that she never intended. That hurt showed up as anger in that moment. That is on me. Those were my thoughts, not hers. The better story, the story I could have chosen to tell myself, is that she does respect me, and her comment was one of concern. She cares about me and wants me to be the best version of myself possible. Had I considered those thoughts first, before reacting, I would have acted better and not hurt her in my response. Fortunately, I did mind my mind shortly afterward, and I quickly went back to her and apologized. I was able to share with her my underlying thoughts; she forgave me, and all is well in the Thompson household once again.

What does all this have to do with Seeing Success, you ask? It's a heads-up warning: the path to an extraordinary life is filled with turmoil, and most of that turmoil is between the ears. The road to getting what you really, really, *really* want has many potholes, detours and roadblocks—and the vast majority are in your mind. Learning to mind your mind, capture thoughts that deter and distract, and choose a better story will increase your velocity toward the results you desire. Much like the efficiency of the brain enabling you to make beautiful music on that guitar, harnessing your thoughts will bring beauty to your life in every way: better relationships and better results. You can have all that you really, really, *really* want, and it starts in your mind. We can, and we must, mind our mind. The stories we tell ourselves can smooth out the road we are traveling on our journey to our success.

PART II
The Seeing Success Formula

SEEING SUCCESS

When you read that phrase–Seeing Success–what comes to mind? Do you see there are a few ways to interpret those two words and the phrase itself? That is very intentional. There are many ways to talk about goal setting and goal achievement, and I started using this phrase after a great deal of interaction with many people striving and struggling to live out their extraordinary lives. I have found that these two words challenge us to think differently from the outset.

First, the term "Seeing Success" is in part referring to future identity. Seeing Success in your life starts in the mind's eye. For you to experience true success, you first must have a strong sense of what it means to you specifically. At least, as specifically as you are able based on your current knowledge and desires. You need to SEE the success that YOU want. You must envision it with as much detail as possible. It cannot be something someone else wants for you, or something you believe others expect. You need to own it, or maybe even better, it needs to own you. You must see it so clearly that you can paint a verbal picture to anyone who asks. And while you are describing it, there should be a bit of excitement churning around in your chest. Maybe even a little fear. That feeling confirms you are headed in the right direction.

Recently, I was talking to a good friend who owns a training company, and after I mentioned my coaching business, he asked me, "What is your coaching like?" The perfect question! I launched into a vivid description of how I challenge my clients to get a picture of what they really, really, *really* want and then work from there. After I spent about three minutes describing my business and my perfect client, he responded excitedly, "How can we work together?"

Because I had spent time "seeing" my business in the future–what I really wanted it to be–I was able to paint a picture of how I help my clients pursue their potential with specific and concise detail so clearly, he "saw" it too. He was then able to envision possibilities about how my coaching business and his training business could benefit each other. What began as just two buddies having dinner turned into a strategic meeting and an acknowledgement to the universe that we were meant to have that conversation. As Dianna Kokoszka, founder and former CEO of MAPS Coaching, says often, "Not every conversation changes a life, but any conversation can." What might have happened, or not happened, if I had not spent the time in advance "seeing" a clear picture of what success in my coaching company looks like?

TAKING AIM

Have you ever shot an arrow from a bow? The mechanics of nocking the arrow and pulling back the string are relatively familiar and easy to do, even the first time you attempt it. Getting ready to release the arrow is pretty much a no-brainer. What is next? What do you need now? Hmm…a target would help, yes? You need to literally see the place where the arrow should go. Seeing Success, in this case, is being able to see the red circle in the middle of the target. It is nearly impossible to hit a bullseye if you don't *see* the target. (I had to say "nearly" only because technically it is possible to hit the bullseye without knowing where it is–but really, do you want to base your success on an extreme longshot?) Once you see the bullseye, you can then aim, adjust for the wind and distance, and act by releasing the arrow. This correlates perfectly with Seeing Success and getting what you really want. It is about getting clear about your life's target, your life's destination. We must SEE success so we can point our lives day by day in the right direction. And because we saw it in our mind first, when we get there, we know we have arrived. Bullseye!

Secondly, the term refers to the "seeing" of your success along the way. Perhaps the most important component in the Seeing Success formula is the constant examination of the activities you are doing and the results you are getting. When you know what you really want, and you have broken that down into action steps and sub-goals, the tracking and measuring of the key metrics are critical to your arriving at success. To continue the bow and arrow analogy, when you miss the center of the target, you can adjust and try again. Each failure to hit the bullseye is an opportunity to learn something, an opportunity to gather more information. Each attempt teaches you a bit more about the wind, the velocity of the arrow in relation to the distance, the angle of ascent and descent, and the mechanics of actually shooting the arrow. You are in the process of seeing: observing the results of each action and improving your skills. You only truly fail if you simply set the bow down and walk away.

The last meaning to Seeing Success is the literal "seeing." When you follow this formula as closely as possible, you will, in time, SEE your own success—the success you really, really, *really* want. Guaranteed!

I would then ask, *Do you want to see success? It starts with seeing success.*

CLARITY IS POWER[4]

The funny thing about seeing is that to see well, you need clarity. I now need glasses to be able to read this on my computer at an average font size. As hard as I try to focus, without my glasses, it is blurry. I need help from a specific piece of glass, strategically placed across the bridge of my nose. Those glasses are bifocals, because when I look up into the distance, I need a different lens to see correctly. The Seeing

4 This phrase is a BOLD Law from Dianna Kokoszka's MAPS coaching program at Keller Williams Realty

Success formula is much like that pair of glasses: each step is like an appropriate lens, helping you see what you need to do more clearly. Each of the four steps helps you focus on the right thing at the right time. You see the target in the distance. You see the path along the way. Adjust as necessary. Bullseye!

As for the word "Success," I need to be very clear about this potentially ambiguous word. Success is what YOU say it is. It must be *FROM* you, not imposed on you. I have coached and mentored young adults, and I've noticed sometimes their definition of success was given to them by a parent, a teacher, or some other figure of authority. Even as adults, we can regard success as something someone else has done and just aim at that.

When I was in the corporate world, I set my sights on the C-suite. From Director to Executive Director, and up the ladder we go. As I got closer, and when I was honest with myself, I realized it really wasn't what I wanted but rather it was the path that was expected for someone in my role. I continued to do the work, but more and more, my heart wasn't in it. I recall a very specific moment in time when I was sitting in the State of the Company monthly meeting with all of the "Cs" of KWRI, literally surrounded by my real estate heroes, and thinking, *What am I doing here?* I remember it vividly–that moment of clarity. I realized I was pursuing goals that were not my own. It was great to succeed in the eyes of others to some degree, and I was being paid well, but deep inside I wasn't satisfied. I could have kept going, but I never would have been truly happy.

I suspect some of you reading this have experienced similar discomfort in a role that seemed right but felt wrong. If that is where you are now, there is hope. The things you learn along the way, even if you discover you are in the wrong role, are still valuable and add to your perspective. Nothing is wasted. I am truly grateful for the corporate experience, the people I was blessed to work with, and all that I learned while in that company. Much of how I think now was influenced by that time spent in a role that wasn't really what I wanted. The good news here is that every exit is also an entrance to something better.

I recall in my second year in the real estate business, a brand-new agent came up to me and said, "My goal is to sell more than you." My first year in real estate I was Rookie of the Year and I was well on my way to breaking more records when he approached me. In that agent's mind, surpassing me was a target that he thought would give him the motivation he needed. Competition works for some, and it can often be a lever to spike your motivation for specific short-term goals. But in the long run, if it is only about winning, it's usually not enough. If there isn't clarity about what you really, really, *really* want long-term, you will eventually lose steam and slump into burnout or boredom. There must be an internal desire to achieve that success you have envisioned in order to maintain the energy it takes to get it. You must take the time to decide what success means to you because when you do, that clarity will provide the energy to sustain the drive towards it. There are no shortcuts here. You must decide, to the best of your ability, with the knowledge you currently have and your current state of awareness, what success means to you. Sometimes it is just to win. And that is fine. But keep looking and examining, and eventually you will envision something bigger than just winning. It's just part of the journey.

By the way, that agent did eventually hit his goal of selling more than I did, only because at the end of my third year, after closing 101 transactions in nine months, I left the industry to follow a call to be a minister at my local church. He went on to own his own real estate sales office, but eventually dropped out and, as far as I know, is no longer involved in real estate at all.

GAINING PERSPECTIVE

Here is more good news: When you decide what success means to you, you are not bound to that vision for the rest of your life; if halfway through the journey you start to change your mind, that is completely fine. In fact, that experience is not uncommon, especially among young adults. Any vision of what success means to you is based on your current perspective and all the things you currently know, believe, and value in *that* moment. If you are just out of high school, your perspective is limited to 18 years of experience. Knowledge increases day by day, and beliefs sometimes change–even core beliefs. You may value adventure and novelty when you are young, but maybe later, after marriage and a few kids, you may value security and time with your family. As time passes, you gain more knowledge and perspective, and yet even then you can only know what you know. Again, you modify your vision of success and start moving towards that goal, and along the way, you gain more insight, more knowledge, more perspective. This is natural, and it is part of the process. The Seeing Success formula remains the path to getting what you really want, but what you want can change, and often, it grows! It is appropriate to take the information you gather along the way and assess whether the success you initially envisioned is still the success you really want. Sometimes it is, and other times it isn't. And either way is okay. When you are aware of this natural process, it takes the pressure off to create the perfect picture of what you really want before you get started, even though the success you envision today is usually in the general direction of the success you will envision a few years from now. Through every small success and failure, you gain more experience and knowledge. Nothing is wasted. Everything is a lesson. Every movement adds to who you are and who you are becoming. You are continuously becoming ***more***! Now THAT is exciting!

The main point here is that being intentional about the direction you are taking your life will give you a life *on* purpose, and a life *with* purpose. Too many have ended up with a life on accident: they started down a path based on a whim or pursued an opportunity that seemed right at the time, and somehow found themselves where they are. And it turned out it wasn't at all what they wanted. How many people do you know who have a degree in one area and a career in an area completely unrelated? It happens more often than it should. It isn't necessarily bad; it is, however, a reflection of how difficult it is to choose a career when you are young and attempting to select a major in college. I recently hired a young lady with a chemistry degree for a sales position. Based on her DISC behavior profile, she is going to be a highly effective agent, and I even asked how she had been able to survive in a lab for the previous seven years. (She replied that she had *only* been surviving.) By the way, at the writing of this book, she has been with us only five months and is absolutely flourishing!

The Seeing Success formula, regardless of where you are in your life right now, will give you the ability to be more intentional. You still may end up in a place you hadn't originally envisioned, in part because what you are imagining now doesn't exist yet. You are creating the life you want. It is uncommon, using the formula, to point yourself in one direction only to find you are going the wrong way. In fact, it is more likely that your life will be better than you imagined! And what is even more exciting is that on your way to the success you see in your long-term vision, you will have more of what you want in the incremental successes along the way. More purpose. More satisfaction. More joy. More.

Notice that the phrase isn't "Being Successful." While this book is definitely about how you are ***being*** in the world and who you are becoming, it all starts with ***seeing***. This formula begins with seeing your success in your mind first, in your thoughts. Because, as I have said numerous times in this book already: Everything starts with a thought. Nothing happens without at least one thought. Make sure it's a good one.

TIME FOR TYPES

One more thing we need to be aware of is our preferred behaviors. You have likely heard of one or more of the many available systems of identifying our personalities and behavior types. Myers-Briggs Type Indicator, Activity Vector Analysis (AVA), Newcastle Personality Assessor (NPA), etc. There are many assessments available to help identify behavior preferences, personality tendencies, even vocational and career choices. In our coaching, as mentioned, we use one of the most well-known behavior tools, the DISC assessment.[5] I will provide just a short overview, and I do recommend that you take a DISC assessment immediately, as well as read a few books on human behavior. This is for the benefit of both knowing yourself and knowing others in order to become more empathetic. It also can increase your effectiveness as a leader, as a boss, as a salesperson, and even as a spouse. Let's just say you can be a better human when you understand human behavior better.

In short, a person identified as a **D** is a driver, dominating, demanding, direct. They can be recognized by their speed, and their apparent ambivalence to others. It isn't that they don't like people, but they just don't necessarily need them, and they sometimes run over people on their way to wherever it is they are going. Not on purpose, mind you–they just don't see them. They find energy by getting alone time. In keeping with our analogy of the Success Journey, I am going to equate the D person to a Porsche. The Porsche is a car designed to go fast. It isn't super flashy, as a Lamborghini or a McLaren, but when one passes you by on the highway, you know you want it.

The person who is identified as an **I** is the influencer, entertainer, center of attention. You know them because if they walk into the room, they already know you somehow, and they know everyone else. They dress to attract attention and they are loud and happy. They gain energy by being with people, and frankly, they need people. They go fast too, but they get distracted by opportunities to have fun. I am equating them to a party bus. They eventually get to where they are going, most of the time, and it is always a lot of fun.

The **S** personality is a steady, calm, thoughtful person. They are the peacemakers, and you may find them saying, "Why can't we just all get along?" They do not like confrontation on any level, and in a room full of people, they might not be noticed as even being there, except

5 DISC assessments are behavioral self-assessment tools based on the 1928 published DISC emotional and behavioral theory of psychologist William Moulton Marston. The tools are designed to predict job performance. The theory describes personality through four claimed central traits: dominance, inducement, submission, and compliance. There are many assessment providers and certifications available.

by a few very good friends they have developed relationships with over time. They move at a slower pace than the D and I, not because they are slow, but because they are more thoughtful and deliberate. They consider everyone else's feelings and in a working situation are typically very reliable and loyal. They are a neutral-colored minivan. Reliable and practical for a variety of situations.

The last major personality identifier is the **C**, which stands for Compliant. They are not compliant in that they comply with others; rather they comply with systems and facts. We may call them the perfectionists of the group. They want everything in their world to comply with how they envision it is supposed to be. They move deliberately and methodically, asking questions and challenging anything outside the norm. They often will not start anything new until they have investigated thoroughly so that they know the right way, so as to avoid mistakes at all costs. They are the Volvo sedans, well-designed and well-built, safe and still reasonably nice looking (from the models built 2010 and after, that is).

Behavior preferences are not as simple as this, but this is a usable framework to leverage as you identify yourself and others. While we all have a combination of the above behaviors, we each have one type that rises above and is our dominant trait. According to the DISC profile developers, there are at least 16 combinations that the majority of humans can be categorized into. As a DI, I go fast, wave at everyone as I speed by, and occasionally stop at parties when it serves my overall goals. As I learned more about myself, I chose to become more empathetic and listen better. It isn't that I am no longer a DI, but I am able to flex my preferred behaviors to align with my values. I believe people are valuable and loved equally by our Creator, and I want to value them, too. And, honestly, that took time on task to improve and gain relational skills. Under pressure, the D part of me steps up front and occasionally runs over those in my path. Yikes! I do publicly apologize to all of you I may have injured.

It is important that you educate yourself in behaviors and even more important that you know yourself. Each personality type will have potholes and roadblocks unique to that profile. The D goes fast, so they miss things and make mistakes. The I gets distracted, and they often do not finish what they start. The S is conflicted and just goes with the flow because they do not want to hurt anyone's feelings. The C far too often just doesn't get going, as they focus on getting ready for so long. Again, human behavior is infinitely more complex and nuanced than these broad strokes suggest, but a cursory understanding of behavior types and personality traits will be of tremendous value as you navigate through traffic on your Success Journey.

CHOOSE BETTER BELIEFS

The biggest pothole of all, regardless of personality and behavior, is the limiting belief. We can call this a mind-block (think: roadblock) in terms of the overall Success Journey analogy. I bet you know what I am talking about. I have met very few who have not had a belief that hinders them. I mentioned the story of learning to play the guitar starting at age 38. When I announced that I was going to teach myself to play, a fair number of nay-sayers cautioned me: "It is very hard to learn an instrument when you are old." (Rude? I know! Thirty-eight isn't old!) I answered, "Only if you believe it is." Since everything starts with a thought, and *belief is simply a thought you have chosen to commit to*, we can take our beliefs captive as well, and choose to believe the truths that set us up for success. If you hear yourself say, "I can't," stop right there! Capture that mind-block and replace it with a better truth: *I may not be able to right now, but I am capable of learning and improving, and I deserve to have what I really want.* This is a truth you must believe, which will empower you to keep pressing forward toward your goals. Limiting beliefs are just that: beliefs. They are just thoughts. We have already established that you are in charge of your thoughts, and you can choose the ones that serve you best. So choose your beliefs carefully.

Without further ado…

...THE FORMULA

The Seeing Success Formula:

1. Goal: Write your Success Vision
2. Plan: Create your Success MAP
3. Schedule: Time-block your Success Schedule
4. Accountability: Identify metrics and track your Success Journey

You might be looking at these four steps and thinking, *Come on, it can't be that simple. I have seen something like that before; that isn't new.* And so on. Maybe you have. But are you currently experiencing the success you know you deserve? No? Do you want more than you currently have? Yes? Keep reading, then. I promise you this formula is different from the myriad of productivity formulas in context and content. The devil is in the details, as they say. (I have no idea who "they" are and why they say that, but they do.)

Every word in the Seeing Success formula is selected precisely to give you clarity about what is expected. Others have chosen different words, and that's fine. Notice the title of the book is "A formula for getting what you really, really want," not "THE formula." I am not claiming that you can succeed only if you follow this formula, only that when you do, you will. If you choose another path, go for it. That said, I am confident that the ideas in this book will challenge you and perhaps cause you to ask better questions, which will get you better answers. Better answers will get you better results. Better results lead to more questions. Rinse and repeat.

The thing about a formula is that you need to follow all of it. It is more like baking than cooking. Let me explain: I love my wife, and she is an amazing cook. She is a feisty Italian with curly blond hair, and eyes that peer into your soul. If you know anything about Italian culture, you know that food is very important. Everything my wife makes is good, and some dishes she makes are amazing! Seriously, she cooks the best lasagna I have ever tasted! No kidding. However, for a very long time, that woman could not bake to save a life. Cookies were hard as rocks, cakes were dry, and I often came home to find another unrecognizable creation. She would just look at me, sort of laughing, sort of crying. Being the coach I am, I finally asked a good question: "Why are you so great at cooking and so horrible at baking?" (Okay, that maybe wasn't the greatest question, but often being direct is the best path.)

She thought about it and then explained that in cooking, she used her intuition, her creativity, and her sense of smell and taste during the process to create a wonderful dish. I asked her if that same creativity worked with baking. She admitted, "Not so far." I asked her what the difference was. "Cooking is a dance with the ingredients. The recipe is often more of a suggestion, or guideline. Baking is more like a science project with a formula. The recipe is exacting and must be followed precisely." I swear to you, the next thing she baked came out perfect, and now she is a great cook AND a great baker. Once she internalized the truth about the need for precision in baking, she was able to bake. Even baking starts in the mind. She now makes some of the very best cupcakes you have ever tasted. Something cool also developed: she decorates them so beautifully, which interestingly satisfies her need for creativity. Clarity gained along the way helped her see that she could still use her creativity–just not during the baking process. Thoughts... beliefs...actions...results.

The Seeing Success formula is a step-by-step recipe, in that you must execute all four steps. There are areas for creativity, and because of the nature of the journey toward your success, there is a *need* for creativity. However, if you skip a step, or perform one of the steps half-heartedly, the cake is ruined. The more you stray from the formula, the longer it will take. All the steps are critical, and as we drill down into each one, you will see none of them are one-and-done, and all of them lean on the others to get you the success you really want. As you read the rest of this book, we will identify some potholes and roadblocks so you can avoid common mistakes and missteps and arrive at the success you really, really REALLY want sooner.

THE SUCCESS JOURNEY

I want to build on the journey analogy that I will return to often as we move through the steps in the following chapters. I have already mentioned potholes, roadblocks, and other references to being on the journey to your success. And we all are familiar with the GPS in your car or on your smartphone. It is interesting that the Global Positioning System follows the four steps above. First, it envisions success when you tell it where you want to go (the Goal). Success is arriving there. In fact, usually, a screen pops up and shows you the destination…sort of, "Did you mean here?" Second, it creates a route (the Plan). After envisioning what success looks like (the destination), and determining your current location, it creates a turn-by-turn plan on how best to get there. Some systems acknowledge that there are options and provide a few choices based on your preferences: fastest, no toll roads, shortest, even scenic routes. Once you select the route, it creates a timeline (the Schedule) by displaying your time of arrival, and your mileage to get there. Along the way, the GPS system keeps track of where you are every second (Accountability). If you miss a turn, it quickly recalculates, creates a new plan, resets the schedule, and keeps watching. Unless you turn it off or simply ignore it, you will get to your destination. You will achieve success. That process, beginning to end, is the **Success Journey**. Just like on any journey you take in your vehicle, anything can happen. In keeping with that analogy, we will talk about potholes, roadblocks, detours, and even rest stops. On your way to your success there will be times when it is appropriate to speed up, slow down, and check your rear-view mirror. The analogy holds, because the journey to what you really want is likely a bumpy and twisty road. Buckle up.

THIS IS LIKE THAT

I am providing this specific analogy to give you something you do know to help you gain a deeper understanding of something you may not know. Remember: our brains are always looking for shortcuts and working to be efficient. Each reader of this book, had I not provided this specific analogy, would have found something they knew and leveraged that knowledge to gain understanding of the Seeing Success formula. I have experienced this pattern with my coaching clients and the students in the classes I have taught. By providing this specific shortcut for them and encouraging them to leverage it as a reminder of the process, I have seen more acceptance and adherence to the formula. Logically, the GPS in my vehicle always directs me to the location that I designate as the goal. In that same way, the Seeing Success formula (**G**oal, **P**lan, **S**chedule + **A**ccountability) will also direct my actions so that I am moving toward the success I have envisioned. It is vitally important that we BELIEVE this truth, as we always act according to what we REALLY believe is true. Belief provides the energy required to move forward toward what we really want despite the obstacles.

BELIEVE THIS

I tell the following story in my classes quite often to illuminate the power of belief. Shortly after getting my license to sell real estate in Texas, I went to a training course called *Sweathogs* by Floyd Wickman. In the very beginning of the course, Floyd introduced the idea of affirmations to us. I hadn't really toyed with affirmations purposefully up to that point, so his suggestion to recite the following statement struck me as odd: "I AM A GREAT REALTOR!" I remember saying it the first time, and it was a bit pathetic: "I am a great realtor?" If I could convey the tonality and intention of that statement, it was more of a puzzled and quirky question than any form of a statement. There was zero commitment. It felt like a lie. Since one of my strongest values is honesty, I struggled to utter the phrase, as I knew I wasn't a great realtor at all. I'd only had my license for about three months and was still running my construction business full-time. But he forced us to say it again. And again. And again. After a few weeks, I could say it with conviction. I committed to saying it every day, and at any moment when I started feeling less than confident. When I chose to focus on real estate sales and let the construction business become secondary, I doubled down on the affirmations, and belief grew. Very quickly, I was, in fact, a great realtor! Believing I was a great realtor, in part, enabled me to close 52 transactions in my first full year in real estate sales.[6] (I went on to close 83 units my second year and 101 my third, and ranked in the top 10 of the San Antonio Business Journal that year.) It all starts in the mind.

The moral of that story is that we CHOOSE our beliefs, and our beliefs matter greatly. We always act on what we really believe. I often said to my youth group when I was a pastor: "If you believe the building is on fire, you will run out of the building." I'll say it again: you act in accordance with what you truly believe.

Beliefs are only thoughts that have taken up residence in your mind. As for the beliefs that don't serve you well, evict them and get better tenants.

Therefore, if you are willing to look at your actions and look for the beliefs behind them, with that awareness you can then choose the beliefs that will best empower you to get what you really want. When you believe in your Goal, you will follow your Plan, and stick to your Schedule. You will embrace Accountability, face the challenges, get back up when you fall, and press on to the abundance you were intended to have. You will have more. You will be more.

TEAMIFY

Most visions ultimately involve other people. If you are building a business, you will have employees, sooner or later. Probably sooner. In real estate, over the last 20 years, teams and groups are more and more common as real estate professionals have begun seeing themselves

6 My average sales price in San Antonio, TX in 1997 was $102K. With 101 transactions, I was ranked number 9 in San Antonio, Texas according to the March 1998 edition of the San Antonio Business Journal. To gain perspective, according to many websites today, in 2022 the average experienced realtor sold 10 to 12 homes per year, and many first-year agents sold 1 or 2. NAR shows average income overall for a realtor in 2022 was $44,813 (www.nar.realtor/agent-income) and much lower for first year agents.

as business owners rather than just realtors. The best businesses are teamified. In other words, each person has a specific role in the overall plan and vision, and they have specific sub-goals within the overall goal of the business. The key metrics of the business are identified and assigned according to the appropriate team member. And here is the most important factor in building and leading a successful team: Each member must fully buy in to the overall vision.

When you, as the leader and owner of the business, cast the vision for where the team is going and what you will be accomplishing, each member must believe in that vision and understand their specific role in moving toward that vision. Their vision for their life must fit within your vision for the team. If they don't believe in what you are pursuing, their performance will likely not measure up. If they don't see how they fit into that vision, they will never be a part of the team in the true sense of *Team*. They may stay and go through the motions, but if they don't believe in you or the vision, they will fail to meet your expectations. The hard truth is that they either *believe or leave*. The unbelievers will frustrate you and confound you regularly. Especially if you like them or, even worse, you are related to them, you will struggle to find a fit for them. But if they don't fit, they don't belong on the team. On the journey to your success, not everyone who starts with you will finish with you. You can only strive to be the best leader you can be, encourage each team member to be the best version of themselves they can be, and hold them accountable to the vision and their role in the plan to succeed. Along the way, with strong accountability, they will either come to believe, or they will leave. Either is okay.

This is the first of several sections of the book labeled *Teamify*. Though the Seeing Success principles apply to both individuals and teams, I'm including these sections to highlight content that is specifically focused on team dynamics and geared toward leaders who are guiding teams of people to success.

CHOOSE WELL

We are all on a journey to the life we will have. We are literally creating our life, day-by-day. What our life looks like at any point on that journey is the sum total of the choices we have made along the way. Just like on a drive, if we don't pay attention, we may end up in the wrong place. If we don't know where we are going, how will we know when we get there? But if we choose to leverage the Seeing Success formula, not only will we get the life we really want, but we will also enjoy the Success Journey along the way. When you can see your success in your mind, and you have a written plan, you can choose well. Things that fit the plan get the thumbs up, and anything that isn't part of the plan gets a hard pass. In addition, our awareness of and attention to our thoughts and actions will cause us to grow as a person and as a professional. Our relationships as well as our businesses will be healthier, stronger, and more satisfying. We can create the life we envision.

MINDSET MATTERS

The following four chapters will dig into the execution of each of the Seeing Success steps. In the last chapter we will look at what it really looks like along the journey–kind of a rubber-meets-the-road chapter. It can be messy, crazy, and chaotic. That is because your old habits will wage war against you, and learning new things sometimes hurts. With the right mindset you can navigate your success, leveraging this formula day by day, time on task. Success is incremental. It is not "one and done." It is a journey filled with potential. That said, the Universe, or God—and I, for what that's worth—want you to enjoy abundance: you can have what you really, really, *really* want.

1. GOAL:
Write Your Success Vision

Yes, I know I do ask this question a lot. It is important: Do you know what you really want? I mean, what you really, really, *really* want? You are in the minority if you are able to answer that with a powerful description of your vision of your future. I have been asking this question of my coaching clients for so long, and I have only had someone answer that question immediately one time–only once out of thousands of times I have asked the question. For those I was blessed to be able to work with, I kept pressing, and kept asking, in every variation of the question I could formulate. When someone was eventually able to give me a clear picture of what they were working for and what they really wanted, everything changed. Everything, every time. When they could really *SEE* what they *really* wanted, the power they needed to get up in the morning and aim their life at their vision showed up. They became unstoppable–literally, a man (or woman) on a mission.

Here is how it all started: I had been coaching for a few years and gotten to the point where I started each initial interview of a new client with, "What do you really want?" Bob (as stated earlier, all my clients in this book will have a version of the name Robert) was a new client, a great guy, and one of the top realtors in his area. He had four employees, and his team was closing about $30 million in volume a year. In the world of real estate, that isn't too shabby. But he was stuck there. As we dug in, I found a lot of activity, but no real direction.

Essentially, he had been selling real estate for about ten years and had gotten into a groove of sorts. (A rut–a nice rut, some would say, but a rut nonetheless.) He was dissatisfied with his current results and decided to get coaching to break through to the next level.

In business, and with any goal worth pursuing, getting to success starts with knowing the starting point, where you are right now. You remember our analogy of the GPS? As soon as you turn on the app, or turn on your vehicle, the GPS shows you where you are. The map pops up, and a blue dot, or an arrow pointer, or a picture of a vehicle shows you exactly where you are. (On my Harley Davidson, the navigation screen displays a black motorcycle 😉.) If the GPS cannot get a signal, it can't do anything. The point is that to start anything, you first need to know where you are. Only then, to get to a certain location, can you enter that address and receive guidance on how best to get there. You can't get there from here if you don't know where *here* is.

Back to Bob. In our first few calls, I was able to get some clarity about where he was currently in his business, but I couldn't get him to describe where he wanted to go. He knew where he was, and he knew he didn't want to stay there. But what did he want? He avoided answering the question. He seemed to always attempt to control the coaching call with the newest fire that needed putting out. He would launch the call with a question about some employee issues, script problems, conversion rates–anything except answering my question: "What do you really want?"

Out of desperation, after three months of him dodging the question, and deflecting to some other "important" matter, I asked, almost yelled: "Bob! What do you really, really, *REALLY* want?"

He stopped cold. Silence. Nothing. It was near the end of the call, and I let him know that his assignment was to have an answer to that question before I next spoke to him and that our next call would not be about anything besides his answer. He seemed off balance, which was very unusual for him. But he reluctantly promised he would work on it.

WORKING ON YOUR BUSINESS

Envisioning your success is hard work. We aren't really taught how to create goals in school, at least not in America. In the schools I have attended, as well as been involved with in various roles, the curriculum does not include, "How to determine your purpose in the world and define the success you want to enjoy." That would be a great class! It doesn't exist, at least not in any typical public school core curriculum. I am asking you to consciously slow down and envision what your life looks like *after* you succeed. If this isn't natural to you, that is okay–you need to do it anyway. I am challenging you to become a visionary!

Think about all of the successful people you see in the news. I am willing to bet that at least one article about them proclaims them to be a visionary. And it is not an exaggeration. Whether it came naturally or not, these men and women envisioned something that hadn't existed before, cast their vision to others, stuck to it, and achieved marvelous things! They got to the top because they saw something others did not. And they were willing to do the work to make it real. Admittedly, some may have a natural bent towards thinking this way, but anyone can learn to be a visionary. It is work, and you can do it if you are willing to do the work. And, if you want success, you *must* do it.

You cannot achieve in real life what you cannot envision in your mind.

The next call, Bob started with, "You know, Danny, I have been thinking about what you asked. You asked, 'What do you really, really, *REALLY* want?'" (Yes, he repeated me exactly, emphasis and all!)

He continued: "I haven't stopped thinking about it all week. I now know, without a doubt, what I really, really, *REALLY* want is...*freedom*."

It was like a huge weight had come off his shoulders and he could now stand up and see more clearly. It was a powerful moment. Up to that point it was like he'd had his head down and was using all his energy just driving the business. Pushing the agenda, pushing his employees, pushing his clients–just pushing. His acknowledgment of what he really wanted seemed to unbind him. His energy changed almost immediately.

We spent the rest of the call talking about what freedom meant to him. I didn't have to ask tough questions. He was ready. He had thought about it all week and had numerous ideas that brought more and more clarity to what freedom exactly meant to him. As he shared his vision, it was as if he was painting a beautiful vision of the future, and I was watching it in real time: first the outlines, then the shapes and colors–slowly becoming a portrait of the life he really wanted. It was wonderful and beautiful to watch him open up and become energized with a clear understanding of why he was working, and what he was working towards. His assignment that following week was to write it all down with as much detail as possible. In our following coaching calls, we continued to develop the clear vision of what freedom looked like to him ultimately, and then worked backwards towards the present to determine what actions needed to be taken to begin the journey toward his success. He broke through his production ceiling that same year and is still growing towards the freedom that he really, really, *REALLY* wants.

THE ROUTE: THE HARD WORK OF VISION

Following is a breakdown of the process to this first step of the Seeing Success formula:

1. Establish your current situation and position in all the areas of your life that matter to you (in whatever order you feel is important to you; it is about what YOU want.) Here are some suggestions:
    a. Your mindset and attitude
    b. Your family
    c. Your health
    d. Your financial health
    e. Your business/career

2. Envision what you really, really, *really* want in each of those areas:
    a. Be as descriptive as possible; paint a word picture.
    b. Make it measurable whenever possible; one way or the other, you need to have a way to measure progress along the way, so you can know when you have arrived.
    c. Write it down and read it back to yourself. Feel it.
    d. Keep rewriting until it is concise and clear, and it makes your heart race.

3. Write your Success Vision Statement
    a. Combine all the things that are important to you from above, and write a Success Vision Statement that describes what the life you really, really, *really* want looks like.
    b. Rewrite it and edit it until it is concise and powerful to you, and it truly paints a picture of what you really, really, *really* want. (No more than three sentences or a page, double spaced.)
    c. Determine how much time it will take you to get there. (Five years is common.[7])
    d. Share it with someone important to you.

4. Post it on the wall where you see it daily.

While that may look daunting, and definitely time-consuming, it is essential that you do the work. In fact, this is the most important work you can do for yourself, for those you are in business with, and for those you love. Know that some areas will be tougher to face than others. Some areas will energize you, and the description will flow freely. Allow yourself to follow your passion and let it flow. Some areas will require hard work. Take your time. This is important. You are establishing the direction of your life. It is worth the investment, whether you do it in one sitting, or it takes you a month, or even longer. I have had clients who take a weekend alone to work on it. One

---

7 I remember hearing Gary Keller say that we are never more than five years away from any goal we choose to set for ourselves. Not sure this is science, but I like it.

of my clients rented a hotel room less than a mile from his home for three days to be able to get quiet and dig deep. Others time-block a few hours each week for multiple weeks. What I have found is that the process has a slow entry point, but once you start to SEE it (remember it's *Seeing* Success), then it comes together more quickly.

Also note that while you are initially identifying all the important areas of your life and seeing success in those areas, you may choose to work hard on only one or two areas at first–and that is fine as well. More on that in Step 2.

THE POTHOLES

1. *I can't get started. I'm stuck. (Typically, the High C and High S personalities)*

If you have never taken the time to really look inside and answer this question of what you want, you may have some scar tissue to get through. Let's be real: the world has beaten up a lot of us. Well, probably all of us in one way or the other. It is not necessarily a smooth highway or a country road when it comes to life in general. Some days feel like we are running uphill against a strong headwind. Sometimes we fall and the world kicks us a few more times for good measure. Sometimes we feel beaten up, and when we look in the mirror, we are the ones wearing the boxing gloves. And sometimes, we find ourselves in a hole that we dug ourselves. Sometimes we were digging that hole because we thought we were actually going somewhere, and other times, we simply wanted to hide.

This is fear, and fear is normal. While fear is not necessarily bad, it can stop you from something good, something necessary. But fear of failure, fear of the unknown, fear of change–these are mind-blocks that can stall us on our Success Journey. Fear originates in the mind, and its source could be myriad things. It could be related to a trauma you experienced in the past; it could be from parental influence; and it could just be from a story you told yourself somewhere in your journey that you now just believe to be true. It could be that you fear what others might think if you really show your heart and begin to move your life toward something different or new, or even risky from their perspective. The point is that fear is only a thought. It's not really real. However fear is manifesting in your life, you need courage to pursue what you really want. Courage is not the absence of fear, but rather the determination to act despite the fear. Courage, too, starts in the mind.

CLARITY PROVIDES COURAGE

If you are experiencing some fear, take a breath, slow down a little, and begin to imagine what your life would look like if you couldn't fail. Imagine what it would look like if everything fell into place. As you create a picture of success in your mind, you are building a place you can go to when you need some courage. When fear creeps in, remember that right now, you are only forming a vision and writing it down. Nothing is carved in stone. You don't have to show it to anyone until you are ready. Take it one step at a time. Worst case scenario: you write a Success Vision Statement and then you throw it in the trash. But what if you take a few steps, and you discover a passion that has been trying to come to the surface of your heart for a long time? What if that small voice inside of you that has been softly encouraging you to go for it were allowed to sing out loud? Take a deep breath and go for it.

This formula can be a ladder to get you out of the hole you have been hiding in. It will get you unstuck, if you are willing to try. It will get you back on course to the life you really want. Fear may have stopped you or slowed you down in the past, but fear is only a thought. It could come from a thought habit you developed over time, but even so, it is only a thought. From that thought you have decided to react in a way that hinders you. It is time to tell yourself another story. Identify the thought and throw it away. Replace it with a better thought that serves you: *What if I couldn't fail?* Wash off the dirt and grime of your past, and stand up and see the abundance all around you. It is all for you. What you want can be yours; you just need to know what you want. The truth is that you are destined for abundance. There is nothing to be afraid of. Take the time to envision what your abundance looks like, muster up some courage, and take the first step toward the life you have always wanted.

2. *I don't know what I want. (Typically, the High I, C and S personalities)*

This one is a shallow pothole. Most of us, before doing an exercise like this, do not know what we want. You are not alone. I remember in a workshop following a class Gary Keller taught to young adults when we were building out KW Kids Can, one student stood up and confessed, "It is so good to know I am not alone. I thought I was the only one who didn't know what I wanted. I thought there was something wrong with me. Now I know the truth. And now I know I can take the first step towards something more. Something bigger."

We were blown away, and it was a reminder to me that as populated and busy as our world is, so many of us feel alone. That, too, is a thought that can hold you back. If you think you are alone, it is another lie you came to believe. You are not alone in this. The world is big, and there are so many options and possibilities. The future is unknown, and deciding a future with ourselves as the hero of our own story is daunting. That said, you can have a future by accident and ignorance (literally ignoring it), or you can design a future that makes your heart pound. You can get what you *get*, or you can get what you *want*, even if you don't know right now exactly what that looks like. Start with something. It will grow.

So then, again, here is the path to discovering what you want when you don't know:

What would you do if you knew you couldn't fail?

Then, just begin.

Know that what you write down at first may not be where you end up. That's fine. It is a process. Everyone else is struggling with this, too. You are not alone. Remember, your destiny is abundance. Maybe right now you feel like you are in a fog, and you don't know what that is. You only know what you know now, and you will know more soon. Each step into the unknown adds to your knowledge and perspective. If you do nothing, nothing happens. Start moving in the direction of something you think you might want and see what you learn. That is so much better than standing still. As you move and gather information and experience new things, you can always re-write your Success Vision Statement. Write it in pencil if you need to. Buy a few erasers. Or, if you are using a computer, save it as "Success Vision Statement version 1." You may revise it as often as you need to. Who cares how many versions you go through before you find *THE VISION* that makes your heart race? That, too, is part of the journey.

3. *I don't deserve more. I don't deserve anything. (Any and all personality types)*

This thought came from somewhere else. Somewhere in your past, you were taught that you should not want a lot, that more was bad. It could be from religion, or from your parents, or it could be just an idea you have come to believe as true. Somewhere along your life journey you started believing the lie that you are not good enough and you don't deserve anything good. I must emphatically state without reservation: BULL!

You ***are made*** for more. The scar tissue of your past may be covering that truth, or it may be that you have determined to bury it with all the platitudes and negative attitudes that others have imposed on you. *Be content with what you have.* Sure, I'm good with that, but that doesn't mean NOT to work for more. Contentment is healthy, but there is also something called *healthy discontent.* We have already established that you cannot know your potential, and the only way to discover it is to aim outward and upward and start moving toward more. Being good *enough* is just wrong. Why are you settling for *less than*? You know what you know now, and you are on your way to knowing more. What you do or don't deserve is not something anyone can judge, because no one knows everything, and frankly, who gives a crap what others think? In my view, there is only one Judge, and He says you are created for an abundant life! In that light, for you NOT to pursue excellence is to shortchange the God who created you, and those you love, as well as yourself. They deserve more from you! YOU deserve more from you! You are created for more!

These lies that say you are not good enough, or that you don't deserve more, are thought habits that are holding you back. It is time to capture the thoughts that are lying to you, name them as lies, and replace them with this truth: *The abundant life is my destiny.* Say it! Say it out loud! *I am made for more!* Repeat this every time you hear the old lie in your head. Affirmations are powerful. You need one or two affirmations to combat each lie. Capture the lie. If you need to see it, write it down on paper and then burn it up. (Please do not do that indoors or in a dry forest.) Write down the truth you are replacing the lie with, and repeat it daily, or more if necessary. Post the truths on your mirror so you see them first thing every day. Put them in your car on the dashboard. Have them posted on your screen saver on your computer. (Do people still do that? I did it for years!) Surround yourself with the truths that will empower you to combat the lies and win a life worth living–the life you really, really, *really* want.

4. *What if I am wrong? (Mostly the High C, but any and all personality types)*

It is possible to write a Success Vision Statement and over time end up somewhere else. True. But what if you are right? What if, after you do all of this hard work, you discover something wonderful? What if, after you scrape off the scar tissue, capture a few thoughts that suck the life out of you, replace them with awesomeness, and climb out of the hole you have become comfortable in, you then find purpose for your life? If you don't try, you won't know. Being wrong is only bad if you then do nothing. Being wrong is part of the process. We only know what we know now, so of course, sometimes we will be wrong. And again, that adds to our knowledge and our perspective, and we move forward again. If you want to learn a lot, be wrong as often and as fast as you can. Think of all you will learn along the way.

5. *I am so distracted (busy, hurt, etc.) I just can't see that far. (Anyone, anytime)*

Here is a portion of text from an email I wrote a few years ago to one of my clients who was feeling this way:

> "Good morning. Just checking in. Any progress?
>
> Capturing a vision for what you really want is often very difficult in the best of circumstances. When things are challenging, it is even harder. It's like being in a fog: sometimes you can see only so far. If that is the case, what can you see? What is the thing that you want that you CAN see clearly? If that is something just a year down the road, or a few months, or even next week, go ahead and get clear about that, for now. Make a plan and focus on that one thing for now. Don't worry too much about the big picture; we will get there eventually. If you have ever driven in a fog, you can only see so far, and when you get there, you can only see so far again, so you keep going. The good news is eventually, you will drive out of the fog. It will lift.
>
> Father[8] has great plans for you."

8 My editor pointed out that this reference to God as "Father" could very well throw some of you off. It's a bit too personal, or maybe your concept of "father" is not a good one. I get it. I work with abused children in a charity I am heavily involved with; I have known some very bad fathers. And, I know the Perfect Father who created everything including you and me. And He loves you more than you can imagine. I know He loves me, and so I endearingly called Him "Father."

Since you don't have to have everything figured out at once, don't let this exercise stress you out even more. Set your sights on the thing you DO know you want, make a plan, and start moving toward that. As you start to get over these mountains (or molehills?), a greater landscape will appear. It is a process. You need to get started. Staying put never made anyone successful, unless their goal was staying put.

6. *I don't know how to get there. (Mostly the High S, but all types are susceptible)*

Another hard truth: None of us really do. The next steps are all about figuring out the route to our success to the best of our current ability. Success is incremental. Do the exercise to the best of your ability and get going on your journey. As you go, you will grow. You will know more and get better at everything you need to get to where you really want to go. So, let's get going.

TEAMIFY

When you are the visionary of the team, this hard work must be done by you. However, you do have a few options. If you have a business partner, then you should do this together. If you have an employee who has been loyal and really meshes with you well, you can invite them into this process. Either way, the over-arching vision must be completed and written out completely so that you can then present it to the team.

THE POTENTIAL

When you take this step seriously and spend the time you need to do it, however much time that ends up taking, it will change your life. It is a necessary investment of time in yourself. I have seen it countless times. Even as I write this, I recall specific moments when clients I had been coaching would break through whatever was blocking their view from seeing their own success. These moments are magical. They are miraculous. They are powerful.

I recall one client, Bobby. (Yep, I will be using every form of Bob I can think of.) Bobby had been in the real estate business for about six years. He was a solid guy, a strong family man; he was devoted to his church and very generous. But his business was mediocre. He had faced some health challenges the year before, and his business had dropped off substantially. That said, he was talented and yet clearly functioning below his potential. The good news was that he knew it. Awareness will motivate you to change and try something different. He decided to try a coach.

"Bobby, what do you really, really, *really* want?"

"Not much. I have most of what I need. My house is paid off, and I have money in the bank. We live simply, and I'm okay with that. I really don't need much."

"I didn't ask, 'What do you need?' I asked, 'What do you really want?'"

And so it went for the first few calls with him. He had settled into mediocrity, living below his potential, and had been telling himself that story long enough that he was beginning to believe it. However, something inside him knew it was a lie, and that's what had prompted him to get into coaching, even though he really had no idea what to expect from it. I am so glad he did.

After asking Bobby many questions, I noticed something that seemed to spark his passion. He was a level-headed guy and somewhat monotone, except when he talked about the mission trips he and his wife had been on in the recent past. There was an underlying passion that showed up each time that topic arose.

"Bobby, what impact do you and your wife make when you go on these mission trips?"

He described the people, feeding the homeless, ministering to the poor, and other vivid interactions with a small number of people, as well as how it made him feel. He felt fulfilled. He felt purpose and meaning. "It fills my heart so much it overflows."

I cannot tell you why I asked this question, but it may have been placed into my mind by Father: "Bobby, what would $50,000 do for that ministry?"

"Oh, man! So many people could be helped. It would change the ministry and increase their impact overnight. So much more can be done."

"Bobby, what does your business need to look like so that by the end of this year, you could write a check for $50,000 to that ministry?"

"Holy smokes! I never thought of that!" And we went on to talk about possibilities and options. His assignment that day was to figure out how much he would need to net in his business to be able to give away $50,000 by December 31. The next week he had a Success Vision Statement, and a plan on how he could get it done. He worked on a schedule, committed to it, and began to execute that schedule and plan with more energy than I had ever seen from him.

I still have the text message he sent to me nine months later. He hit his goal early. Not twelve months later. Nine. And that ministry he cared so deeply about will never be the same.

What YOU really, really, *really* want may not be directly about you. It may not be what is expected of you. It may seem weird to others, and it may make you uncomfortable. It may seem impossible. None of that matters.

What do you really, really, *really* want? Answer that question, and you—and your world—will never be the same.

2. PLAN:
Create Your Success Map

A few years ago, I was invited to a meeting where the gentleman presenting shared a very large vision for an organization he was preparing to launch. He had slides and a packet, and it was impressive. It was big. Like most presentations, you can only say so much in 60 minutes, so I left with some questions. Overall, I saw real potential. Later, I asked for a short meeting with him, where I let him know I saw lots of possibilities, and I may be interested in being a part of it. "I enjoyed your presentation. I see how big your vision is, and it is exciting. I'd like to know, what is your plan to make it happen?"

"I don't know."

That was not what I expected. I understand the concept of setting big goals. I worked for a man who was famous for saying, "What if we double it?" As annoying as that can be, that same man also said, "The purpose of a goal is to make a plan." Now that is brilliant. Think about that for a minute: The only reason you need a goal is so that you can create a plan on how you will hit that goal. Once you have devised a plan, the goal is eye candy. The goal becomes the reminder, the WHY, the energizer, the target. Yes, when we are going somewhere, we absolutely need to know where that *somewhere* is. Hence, Step 1: Write Your Success Vision. You must have clarity about your goal. Now, we need clarity about the path to that goal. We need to know the answers to: *How do I get there? What do I do now? What's next?* And even, *Why am I doing this?* In our GPS analogy, after we enter the destination, we wait for it to create the route–the plan. Then, and only then, we can start moving toward the destination. In the case of Seeing Success, creating that plan is on us.

A VISION WITHOUT A PLAN IS A WISH

Creating a plan will feel like work. Only because it is. That said, I have found that for most people, once they have a powerful vision that truly excites them, creating a plan happens relatively fast. When you see where you are going up ahead of you, you can usually figure out how to get there. And as long as you keep the goal in mind and you continue to see it ahead, as you start moving towards that goal, you can adjust, alter your course, and keep moving.

Robert had a decent business. After only four years, he was in the top 20 producers in his office. He came out of another industry unrelated to sales, and he just jumped in. He was talented and motivated, so he did well. He wanted to grow his business, because you are supposed to grow. That was normal, right? But truth be known, he was just winging it. After several calls with me pushing him to tell me what he really wanted, he blurted out, "I want a Ford Raptor!"

I replied, "DUDE! I love those trucks! When do you want it?" I knew he could go buy it today on credit, so I added, "What if you paid cash for it?"

He was quiet for a few seconds and said, "I thought you were going to tell me that was weird. I'm not like everyone else." He went on to explain that he didn't fit into the box of the typical real estate professional. He didn't want the big house and all the flashy stuff. He just wanted a cool truck.

I explained, "Robert. This isn't about what anyone else thinks. This isn't about what anyone else wants. This is about you and only you. Now that we know you want a Raptor, let's make a plan to get it. What else do you want? That is your assignment for the next call.

Write down everything you really want, and let's start working on the plans to make it happen."

In the next few days, Robert had a breakthrough. Before the next call, I received several emails with numerous attachments. I vividly remember one page in particular. It had a circle with his family in the middle, and he had drawn circles all around it in various sizes, various distances from the family circle. Across the top he had written, "By the time I am 40." It was beautiful! This was a picture of his goals: what he saw himself achieving, what success meant to him. He also sent me his plan. He broke down the sub-goals for that year, and the activities he was committing to do to get there. He shared the strategies he determined he would need to leverage, as well as the metrics he would track along the way. On our call, he explained that it all came together once he knew what he wanted. Once he was allowed to dream his *own* dream, he was free to want what he *really* wanted. That clarity led to more clarity.

That day was the beginning of a journey leading him to *his* success. Once he was set free to envision what he really wanted, the vision showed up. With that vision that lit him on fire, the plan poured out. Did we know the plan would absolutely work? Nope. But based on what we did know, we knew it would definitely get him closer, sooner, than if he just kept doing what he had been doing: winging it.

TEAMIFY

If you lead a team, this is a great time to get them involved. You must cast your vision to them and show them where you are taking them. If they are the right people, they will get excited, too. They will have ideas about what it will look like for them, and they will have input on how to get there. They may push back or ask questions that may be tough for you to answer with total clarity. That is okay, and actually it is healthy for you to consider those questions. This activity will add to your perspective, challenge you to think of things differently, and open your mind to options and opportunities you may not have considered. In my experience, you might even discover the goal will be easier to reach than you originally thought.

One other thing: you may find someone on your team who doesn't fit. We already talked about this, and I wanted to remind you to watch for it during this step. They may not catch the vision. They may not see themselves in the future you share with them. This, too, is okay, and can even be a blessing in disguise. When I was a pastor, sometimes a congregant would choose to leave to go to another church. We often called these departures *blessed subtractions*. That may sound harsh, but if someone isn't growing, and isn't happy on your team, there is a place that will be better for them out there somewhere. Helping them find their next opportunity is often the kindest thing you can do for them.

The act of casting your Success Vision to your team or to your spouse or your coach–even to an unsuspecting stranger you happen to meet–is always good. It adds color to your rough draft. The more you talk about it and hear yourself say it, the more deeply it is embedded into your mind, and the clearer the vision gets. Along the way, you may add or remove parts of it, and craft it into the perfect view of your future success. In your Success Journey, this is the roadmap, the navigational display of the path you will take to get what you really, really, *really* want.

THE ROUTE: THE PATH TO SUCCESS

1. Determine the time period for the goal you have envisioned.
   a. Try five years and think about how that feels. Does it scare you a bit? Does it seem impossible? That's okay; you can always adjust later. Remember, we don't KNOW the future, but we can certainly have a say-so about what it will be!
   b. Does five years seem too easy? Double the goal and see how that feels. Remember, we only know what we know now, and we will know more in the future. Don't sell yourself too short. (We will discuss this further below.)

2. Determine, based on that time period, what your goals should be for **this** year:
   a. Use the Success MAP[9] tool to enumerate strategies and tactics that will be leveraged to accomplish this year's goals.
   b. Use TIMELINE BRAINSTORM to break everything down into priorities and a timeline (optional, depending on the complexity of the plan).
   c. Envision how that will feel when you reach these goals on December 31.

3. Determine measurable goals that will be tracked along the way; be very specific.
   a. List all metrics for the end of the year.
   b. If you have a team, break down who is responsible for each metric.
   c. Break down those metrics for each month, week and day.
   d. Write them down and post them where you see them constantly. Share them with your team and your coach

9 MAP is an acronym for My Action Plan.

THE TOOLBOX

Tool 1: The Double-it Tool

A while back, I was presenting a plan to Gary Keller about KW Kids Can and the online platform I was going to create. And he was into it. I had a presentation, and I was clicking pages on my PowerPoint and sharing my ideas and vision. I saw he was excited, and so I got more excited; we were jazzed! Suddenly, he stopped, and his countenance changed.

Abruptly, he said, "What if we double it?"

I was dumbfounded. Two seconds before that, he had been urging me on; he'd even grabbed the mouse, clicking and looking and saying, "Cool, cool, cool." Now I was staring at him staring at me with the challenge of doubling a plan I had worked on for over a month.

"I'm not sure I know how to double it."

"Then I guess you have some work to do." That was the end of that meeting.

At first, I chalked up Gary's response to the fact that he was one of those people who never seemed to be satisfied. Why does he always ask us to double everything? I had heard him say "Double it" several times in the six years I worked with him, to me and others, and I'm pretty sure I wasn't the only one annoyed by it. I knew him well enough to know that he always pushed himself, and he always expected everyone's best, but why always "Double it"?

I remember vividly the day Gary and I were in his office just talking about life. We had been talking about the early days of Keller Williams, and at some point, I asked why he had structured the regions the way he did. Instead of answering, he asked, "Why do you think I did it that way?" And then he added, "Don't think like you; think like me."

I stopped, and somehow, I adjusted my view; to the best of my ability, I put myself in his shoes and looked at the world from his perspective. I replied, "So when the leaders win, you win."

He smiled and leaned back, quite satisfied with himself, and said, "Exactly."

I have told that story before and some people conclude that his response to me came from a place of arrogance. I don't think so at all. That was a gift that keeps on giving. If we always think like us–viewing things only from our limited perspectives–we will always see what we see. We will always choose what we choose. If we are willing to think bigger, we will see bigger, choose bigger. The thing about thought habits is that they can keep us caged. So, after some intentional thought about the *double-it* habit, I realized that it was a habit that Gary had intentionally grown in his mode of operation. He wasn't being mean. It wasn't that he believes everyone always aims too low. He simply knew that any goal we make is based on what we currently know, and the discipline (or habit) of asking, *What if we double it?* is a tool to challenge ourselves to think beyond what we know, beyond what we are thinking in that moment. It gets us out of our comfort zone. Think about it: A bigger goal makes us write a bigger plan. A bigger plan will get bigger results. And, even if we don't hit the bigger goal, very often our results are better than the original plan had even hoped for. So thanks, Gary.

The discipline of the Double-it tool is to help you make sure you aren't aiming too low or settling for *less-than*. Here is how it works:

Write the goal. Make the plan. If it doesn't scare you a little, go back and double the goal.

If you attempt to make a plan on the doubled goal, and you just can't figure it out, that goal may be too big. And that is okay, too. Lower the goal a little and see if you can create a plan with the goal a little lower. The actual act of writing a plan, a plan that makes sense and one that you are willing to execute to the best of your ability, is one of the determining factors of understanding whether you should actually attempt it.

By increasing the goal, or doubling it, you are forced to think differently, to think bigger than is natural for you. And that is a very good thing. Once you have a plan that makes you nervous, but you are pretty sure you can accomplish, then you have hit the sweet spot. A good plan excites you and scares you at the same time. All you need then is a little courage to push through the challenges you will certainly face along the way. It always takes courage to move into the unknown. The unknown will always have some turmoil. Embrace it! Your success is on the other side of that turmoil.

Tool 2: Success MAP–My Action Plan*

The plan itself, the Success MAP, should be on one page—just one page—and should include the following:

- *End of Year Goal (EOY): Your Destination*

When you envisioned what you really want, and started the planning process, you determined what the goals were for this year based on the Success Vision. The one-year plan is best done in October or November in preparation for the following year. From now on, do it that way. But for now, do it right now, regardless of what date it is, and set the goal for the end of this year. Write out the goal in one or two sentences at the top of the page. It should be very clear what your intentions are. If it is a dollar amount, be clear about whether it is gross revenue, or net, and whether it is a team goal, or a personal goal. Be certain to draw a clear and concise word picture of where you want to be at the end of the year, or the specific time frame you have chosen.

If the sentence is incredibly long or unclear, keep working on it. Review the Success Vision Statement you wrote earlier, and make sure the current goal is on the route to that success. If you have something in the goal that doesn't belong, remove it. If something is missing, and you need some incremental movement this year, add it. Edit it until it makes sense and until you are willing to commit to it. The *willingness* to commit to it is critical.

- *Absolutes: Your Route*

List the sub-goals within the stated goal that must absolutely be completed by the end of the year. There should be two to four absolutes that will define the metrics that must be hit in order to ensure the goal for the year is completed. For example, a loan officer may include the number of loans closed, the number of clients added to a database, and the date by which an assistant will be hired. An insurance agent may track gross commission or policies in force, and the number of referral partners. Most real estate professionals track gross commission income and the number of listings and buyer contracts. Everyone should also include a specific number of educational or professional development events to attend, as well as a two-week vacation. (Yes–include growth and personal goals. If you don't, it won't happen.)

To get started, write down every absolute you can think of. Then review and ask yourself, *Is this something absolutely necessary for me to focus on to hit my goal this year?* Be brutal. If the answer isn't a resounding *Yes!* then scratch it out. Limit yourself to four absolutes at most, because the truth of the matter is that when you attempt to focus on too many things, you go cross-eyed. Truthfully, even four is pushing it, but I have worked with enough people to know some of you will want four absolutes. Three is better. I need to encourage you to spend the time it takes to get this right. Remember, when you follow the Seeing Success formula, this is the "calculating" part of the GPS analogy, the *mapping out* of the Journey. This will determine specifically what you must focus on for the next 12 months. It is worth the time it takes to get it as right as you know how. Once you have edited and re-written this map and it absolutely lists the things you must focus on to get to where you want to go, write them down, numbered 1 through 3 (or 4) below the EOY goal statement. Every one of the absolutes must be measurable, checkbox-able. If it can't be measured, and completed, it can't be an absolute.

▸ *Tactics: Your Tools and Activities*

Take your first absolute and start writing all of the activities required to complete that particular absolute. Considering the hypothetical real estate agent's absolutes above, "number of listings closed," he may designate these activities as part of his strategy:

- Call sphere of influence two hours each day.
- Mail marketing letter to every expired listing in this neighborhood.
- Hold one buyer seminar each month.

Go ahead; write them all down.

Once you finish the first absolute, do the same activity for the next one, and the next. Once you have exhausted your ideas, go back and identify the tactics that will make the biggest impact toward completing each absolute, and prioritize them. You can have no more than six for each absolute, but three or four is better. It is very important that you make certain the activities are the *right* activities to move you toward the absolutes. You are establishing how you are going to spend your days working. As I stated before, this is worth the time investment. Not only are you choosing what you will be doing, but you are also choosing what you will NOT be doing.

The point of this tool is to gain clarity. There are many business planning tools out there, and in fact, this one is a culmination of tools I have used over the years. KW's 1-3-5 tool (also known as GPS for Goals, Priorities, and Strategies) is a fantastic tool, and is probably the one I used the most, and where I learned that having it on one page only is a powerful way to gain clarity. If you have a planning tool that already works for you, use that. This is not about me; it is about you. If you fail to plan your business, as they say, you are simply planning to fail.

This plan will empower you to make absolutely certain every activity you do each day is moving you closer to your goal. Efficiency is freedom. Again, as before, every one of the tactics must be check-box-able. If it is ambiguous, and you cannot find a way to at some point say, *This is done*, then it doesn't belong on the list. And don't list obvious things, such as "Do my taxes." That isn't a tactic; it is a chore that is required if you live in America. Stick to the imperative activities you must do to accomplish the absolutes. If any of your absolutes have no tactics, then it IS a tactic, not an absolute.

▸ *Potholes and Roadblocks*

The list of potholes and roadblocks goes on a second page, and it is very different from the Success MAP. The Success MAP is a concise, single-page document that you will post and share in several places: post it on your office wall and on your desk; share it with your team and your coach. It's a public document of sorts. But the potholes and roadblocks list is to go into your desk drawer, tucked away, just in case. Write a short list of the potholes and roadblocks you are likely to face, with a tactic of how you will face each problem. This is sort of a Boy Scout exercise. You know their motto: *Always be prepared.* This exercise is a way for you to be as prepared as you possibly can to face the roadblocks and potholes of this journey you are about to embark on. In a sense, thinking through the problems and identifying the options and possible solutions is like packing the jack, spare tire, and flares in the trunk of your car. And maybe some other tools, just in case. You may not need them, but if you do, you will be very glad you spent the time packing them.

You know *you.* Write down the problems you may face on the day-to-day journey toward success this year. We mentioned the boredom; is that a problem for you? If so, how can you best deal with it? Write that down. A client of one of my coaching buddies had a goal of calling potential clients three hours each day with a goal of taking at least one listing appointment. He found himself looking for other things to do, and he would find reasons to leave his office before the work was done. To overcome this pothole, he decided that when he got to the office each morning, he would remove his pants and shoes and set them outside his door; his assistant would then take the pants and shoes, placing them on the other side of her office. Her directive was that he could not have them back until he had a confirmed valid appointment. Sometimes he was done early, but other times, he spent longer than three hours calling. He made a commitment to his goals, and his distractions kept getting in the way. So, off with his pants! At times, that is what commitment and preparation look like. All I can say is it was a good thing he had blinds on his window.

My first year in my real estate business, because I am easily distracted, I hung a sign on my office door that said, "If this door is closed, do NOT disturb." Apparently, that ruffled some people's feathers, as a month or so later I noticed a sign on one of the other realtor's doors: "Open or closed, come on in!" I am just wondering who was laughing when at the end of that year I sold three times as much as he did, and he had been in the business for over seven years. (Did I mention I can be an a-hole at times?)

Think it through. What might trip you up? What if the market shifts? What if there is another pandemic? What if interest rates jump? What if there is a major storm that disrupts normal activities in your area? If you live in Tucson, Arizona, that probably won't happen, but if you live in New Orleans, Louisiana, or almost anywhere in Florida, this is a good thing to at least consider. Think about the big things and the little things. Let's say you have several hours each workday prospecting for business, door-knocking or on the phone. What if you get hungry or thirsty? Bring energy bars, snacks, and water bottles. Are emails or incoming phone calls going to distract you? Leave your phone in another room or turn it off. (God forbid!) Close your email software. Will you struggle setting appointments with new referral partners? What can you do to make sure you overcome the internal resistance and stick to the plan?

The point of this exercise is to just spend some time thinking through issues you may encounter: your own personal roadblocks, potholes, and detours. The outcome of this exercise is that, when you go back and reread it, you will realize that you really don't have any major obstacles to your success. You may identify a pothole or roadblock that you can start planning for now, instead of getting stuck later. You may discover there is a specific skill you need to learn, or some knowledge you need to gain. You may need to go back to the tactics and add a book to read, an event to go to, or a training program you need to sign up for. The good news is that the vast majority of the difficulties you may face have easy solutions, especially if you have taken the time in advance to think them through. This will build your confidence. Confidence is not the knowledge that you know everything and can do anything, but it is knowing that you are prepared and able to figure out anything you encounter along the way. You are ready to recalculate when necessary, and you will have what you really, really, *really* want.

TEAMIFY

When you are leading a team, the company has an overarching Success MAP, and each person has their own MAP, and all of the MAPs must align with the company's MAP. Yes, that feels like a lot of work. Do you really, really, *really* want your success? Buckle down, time-block, and do the work. It pays off; I promise.

Tool 3: Timeline Brainstorm

Many times, during the planning process, you may find it difficult to prioritize. The timeline brainstorm tool will help identify the order of activities to be performed; it is especially helpful with a team and with a plan or complex project with a lot of moving parts. I learned this many years ago at a Church Multiplication training course and have used it countless times to break down my year into manageable increments. I have used it for special projects to gain clarity about the timeline needed to succeed. I even used it a few months ago when my training manager and I were writing a training program for onboarding new agents. Whether you are launching a business, working on a large project at your job, or trying to grow your existing business, often you will need new systems and new team members along the way, which in turn demands new systems again. Clarity leads to success. The process is as follows:

Use a room with a large whiteboard or a large window that you can use dry erase markers on. You will also need pens and sticky notes. Depending on your project/plan, you may need eight to ten feet of space on which you first draw a straight line across the top. Write the months of the year across that line starting on the left, January through December (or whatever the timeline is). Gather your team members into the room. (If that is just you, it's all good. If you have a very large team, gather only the leaders.) Everyone gets a sticky notepad and a pen. Remind everyone of the vision for the year, and even the long-term Success Vision Statement, if appropriate. Now you are ready.

Each person will begin by writing any activity or task that needs to be done on a sticky note, then placing it on the wall under whichever month they guess it might need to be completed by. I say *guess* because for now, the time frame might not be knowable yet. Don't worry; it can be moved later–hence the sticky notes. Just get it written and get it on the wall.

As an alternative, each person can call out the task, activity, event, whatever, and a designated writer can add them to the whiteboard. (I do it this way because my handwriting is so bad, I cannot read what I have written.) Keep going until no one can think of any other activity or task that needs to be completed. Example tasks that might be added are: hire new admin, complete database conversion, buy new laptop, go to this event, have this client event, etc. These are not the daily activities that must be done, but tasks that need to be completed along the way to your success. At this stage of the exercise, write everything without a filter; the idea is to get all potential ideas–good and bad–in one place. Be sure the format you choose allows everyone to share their thoughts out loud, as an idea one person suggests may cause someone else to think of another task that needs to be done before or after that. If you have big plans, you might need a lot of sticky notes. I always use one color, but you can use different colors for different departments. Adapt the activity to suit your specific situation, and try having some fun with this.

Next, when no one can think of anything else, read through all suggestions. Start moving the items that have a very specific date to the appropriate place under the timeline. For instance, if you are taking your team to a conference on May 15, place it on the timeline close to the line, as it is immovable. Because the conference is in May, the tickets to the event and the flights and hotels need to be secured when? Move that note over to the appropriate date. If it is a task, place it at the time it needs to be completed. With some larger tasks, a start date may need to be identified. Hiring someone by July may mean interviewing starts in March, and posting the position must occur in February. Keep moving the notes around until the sequence of activities and tasks makes sense. When you all step back from the wall, you will see the plan in a step-by-step action plan in that sea of sticky notes.

Once the timeline makes sense, discuss with the team who is responsible for what. If you *are* the team, that will be easy: you do it all. If you have a large team, the leaders who have employees reporting to them will take responsibility for their team's activities and tasks. Mark the notes accordingly: have each person initial the tasks for which they are responsible. Every note should have an initial.

At this point, you will have clarity about what it will take to implement your plan. You will see whether certain months are too busy, or certain others have a lull. You may be able to move things around and smooth them out a bit. You may find one team has too many burdens, and you may be able to adjust who does what. You may determine you have to hire another person, get another office, buy more equipment. This timeline will identify any gaps in your plan, as well as illuminate whether the goal is too big or too small. Lastly, converting this to a spreadsheet, color-coded for each person and printed and posted on the wall, is a very powerful reminder for you and the team to stay on track. Each member should have a copy near their desk, workstation, or office.

When I launched a national non-profit educational program, KW Kids Can, my team and I spent half a day working through our timeline. We had hard-date events that had to happen, which determined when workbooks had to be printed, which then helped us recognize when content had to be written. We then knew we needed to find software that would allow registration for the events, which caused us to see we had to build a proprietary site. This exercise allowed us to see the entire year in one moment and revealed any weakness in our plan. It gave us crystal clear clarity about what we had to do and when we had to do it. We each had the timeline color-coded and displayed in our office so we could refer to it often. If some task or event were delayed or changed, we made the necessary adjustments. Because we took the time to plan the year–and kept our eye on the plan—we had a fantastic year. Honestly, fan-freakin-tastic.

By leveraging this tool, you will always know where you are on your journey. You will always know who is responsible for doing what and when. You will know sooner than later if adjustments need to be made. In some ways, this is the dashboard of your success vehicle. With it, you are able to monitor the systems and critical components of the plan during the journey. As long as you look at them regularly, you can know the health of your vehicle and determine where you are on your journey to success.

THE POTHOLES

1. *I can't get the plan to fit on one page. (C, I)*

Try harder. You need to get it to one page. This is non-negotiable. The truth is that a complicated plan rarely succeeds. If it doesn't fit on one page, your stated goal is too vague or ambiguous. Look over your sentences. Can they be more concise? Review each absolute. Is it really absolutely necessary? Is every tactic and activity absolutely necessary to accomplish the goal?

As stated earlier, it is important to be brutally honest with the plan. I once had a client provide me with a six-page plan. He decided his way was better and refused to edit it down. As brilliant as he was, he did not get it all done, and frankly, could have had a much better year had he focused on fewer things. He spent too much time on tasks that were not necessary for the goal he had set for himself. Gary Keller has on the title page of his best-selling book *The One Thing* an old Russian proverb: *If you chase two rabbits, you'll catch none.* You don't need complicated; you need clear.

Take a little more time, and force yourself to ruthlessly eliminate whatever you must so that you only have one page. This will force you to prioritize. Once you have done this refining, the result will be that you will give more focus to fewer things and will be able to do them better with less distraction. You may need to consider your behavior profile. The high C (compliant, perfectionist) will struggle with this the most, desiring to include every detail on the plan in hopes of being specific and thorough. But that is not what the Success MAP is; it is intended to be a one-page plan that you can look at daily, and that everyone on your team can refer to daily, so that the priorities are always in sharp focus, and the distractions are identified for what they are. This is not to be a step-by-step playbook, but a specific tool to keep you focused on your success. (Cs love the timeline exercise, so do that.)

2. *How do I know whether this plan is big enough to get me to my five-year goal? (S and C)*

Truthfully, you don't. Stick to the process, and do the work. None of us know the future, but we do have a say in what we do as we go there. Envision your success, break it down to this year, make the plan, double it, and make the plan again, until it excites you and scares you. That's it. Don't make it complicated, and don't second-guess yourself. On this journey to your success, there will be potholes you didn't see, roadblocks and detours you hadn't accounted for. Mind-blocks will be uncovered. AND there will be successes that were easier than you expected, things that went perfectly, and wonderful surprises as well. Add to that, nothing is written in stone. We can change the plan. We can change the goal. We will grow as a person and a leader. What we ***can't*** do is wing it and expect to get what we really, really, *really* want.

3. *There are things on this plan that I do not know how to do. (S, C and sometimes I)*

Awesome! That means it is a very good plan. Identify each task you do not currently know how to do, and determine whether you are going to ***learn it*** or ***leverage it.*** Some things the leader needs to do. So then learn it. Buy a book today. Find someone who knows it well and talk to them. See if there is something you can work out with them to grow your knowledge and/or skill. Find a class, seminar, workshop, whatever. Make a plan and go learn it.

If you don't have time to learn a new skill, or don't really need to know it for long-term growth and success of your plan, leverage it. Is there a system you can purchase that automates the activity? Do the research, talk to others who are using it, and buy it if it makes sense and fits in with your plan. Or pay someone. Start with a virtual assistant or contract labor rather than an hourly employee if you don't have any employees yet. Being an employer is an entirely new skill as well. In the real estate world, the first point of leverage is usually the transaction coordinator. The most time consuming part of the business is the contract-to-close documentation. In most states, a realtor can pay someone $400 to handle it better than they can. Pay that person per contract, and then take those 30 hours you get back to go find more buyers and sellers to work with. In the mortgage business, it's common to have an assistant or even an LOA (Loan Officer Assistant), similar to a mentor process. The pay can be contractual, based on results, rather than hourly. I am using a similar model in the insurance agency, teaming up a senior producer with a newbie. The point here is that tried-and-true growth models don't require taking on a full-time employee too soon.

If you are going to hire someone, be sure to learn about being a boss first. It is harder than it looks. That said, having a team of motivated talent whose vision for their life fits into your vision for your life is a wonderful experience. That is a huge topic, and we don't have time for that here. There are many books and training events to help you grow those skills. Make sure you add them to your plan. Maybe that's my next book.

4. *Half the year is gone; I'll just wait till next year to plan. (D, C, I)*

No. Start now. Do not wait. This process does not require you to wait until October and plan for a full year. In fact, you can use this process for small and short-term projects. The timeline can be any time you choose, and the process is exactly the same. Be specific about the goal and specific about the time; it can be 90 days or a year. When I learned to play guitar, I wrote out my goal, decided six months was what I needed to commit to, and wrote a six-month plan. I implemented it, and in six months I played guitar. Stop procrastinating and making excuses. Do the work, and go get what you really want. It's out there waiting for you.

THE POTENTIAL

When you enter your destination into your GPS, it comes up with a plan and typically asks, "Is this the route you want to go?" Often, depending on the software, you have a few choices. You choose the plan based on where you want to go and how fast you want to get there. This step is exactly that. You are determining the route to your success. You are mapping it out and choosing, to the best of your current ability and knowledge, how you want to get there. Since you have never been there before, much of it is a guess. You may have the luxury of using similar past experiences to give you insight, and you can engage an expert, a coach, or your team members to add to your perspective and to help you make good choices. You don't have to do this alone, and frankly, you probably shouldn't. Regardless, you must make a Success MAP. As I stated earlier, a vision without a plan is a wish.

Gary Keller, who literally launched and built the largest real estate company to ever exist on the planet, recently said this: "As I reflect, this is not the company I envisioned when I created Keller Williams; it's so much more." He, with the assistance of a lot of other talented people along the way, kept envisioning, making plans, acting, re-envisioning, making new plans, and acting–for over 30 years. With many failures along the way, Gary was able to recalculate his path as he grew in knowledge, experience, and awareness, until the company he led became much, much more than he had originally imagined. And that is how it works. He finished that statement by adding, "I am proud and honored to be your leader and look forward to what the future holds." He isn't done yet. I dare say this is how it always works.

Make your plan and remain flexible because the universe has great plans for you.

You do the work, the plan takes shape, and you post it on every wall you own. What happens next? We will be discussing "Set Your Schedule" next, and that will answer this question with a resounding, *Take a step. Then another. Then another.* By leveraging the entirety of this formula, you will know exactly what to do next. It is a turn-by-turn plan toward the life you really want. The power in the Success Mapping process is two-fold: It colors in the sketch of your Success Vision in more vivid detail, giving you a deeper sense of how to get what you want; and it provides a solid framework by which to judge every activity as a *Yes, I need to do this*, or a *No, I cannot spend time on this*. It provides you with clarity and helps you increase efficiency. This, then, brings your success into view, and what you really, really, *really* want is within your grasp. Let's move on to the next step.

3. SCHEDULE: *Time-Block Your Success Schedule*

You've probably often heard people comment in frustration, "There just isn't enough time in the day!" In fact, you've probably often said it yourself. It has a truthy feel to it, but we all know that time is the same for everyone, and the day always has 24 hours, every day. We can set our clocks to it. In fact, we do set our clocks to it. Yet, we all know someone who seems consistently to get more done each day. I am willing to bet that person has a written schedule. Whether they follow something like what we are about to discuss, or some other form of it, one way or another, they have discovered that you cannot make the day longer, you can only make the day better. You cannot create more hours in the day and so your only path to getting more done is setting a schedule of the right activities at the right time and sticking to it. In a word: efficiency. If you want to get what you really want, the fastest path is the Success Schedule.

Of the four steps, this is the one where I get the most pushback. The vast majority of clients I have worked with are naturally very entrepreneurial. They are mavericks who enjoy the freedom of doing what they want each day, of not having a boss. I joke a bit that many entrepreneurs are unemployable, which is why they pursue building their own business. They have to–no one would hire them. Their desire for freedom overcomes their fear of the uncertainty of launching something that is their own. Even though they usually have routines and day-to-day habits that might appear to be a schedule of sorts, when I ask them to do so, they hesitate to write out a schedule and post it on the wall where everyone can see. Most responses to my request to write out a repeatable, weekly schedule in advance go something like this: *How can I make a schedule? I don't know what might come up. I might need to do something that's not on that schedule.* Or, *A schedule like that feels restrictive. I got into this business to be able to do what I want.* And, when a client with a similar perspective complies and writes the schedule, not fully believing it will work, they rarely stick to it. This, too, is a mindset issue and starts with belief. Right now, I am challenging you to believe that a schedule will bring focus to your life, make you more efficient, and get you to your success faster than any other method. I am suggesting that you write out a daily schedule, starting from the time you must get up until the time you need to be in bed, in great detail, post it for all to see, and entitle it, "My Boss."

I may have just lost you. My response to a common gut reaction of "Forget this crap! I'm out!" is "That's too bad. It would have been awesome to see you achieve your success faster and more efficiently with much less stress."

TRUE FREEDOM HAS A SCHEDULE

So, you decided to read at least a bit more, did you? Good. I promise that as uncomfortable as this step might feel to you now, in time, you will find that creating a schedule is actually the most freeing thing you can do. Determining the perfect schedule for your most productive day and following it as if it were your boss is one of the most powerful practices you can engage in for your business. And everyone around you will love you more for it. Your team will be glad to know where you are and how what you are doing at any given time fits into that Success Vision you are so passionate about, the vision they bought into. Your customers will appreciate you because they can rely on you to do what you said you were going to do when they decided to do business with you. And, your loved ones will be happy to see you regularly because when you follow your schedule, you will have the time off you scheduled, days and vacations where you don't look at your phone or email. REAL days off. I cannot tell you how many potential coaching clients I have interviewed who have told me they do not remember a day off when they didn't answer the phone, deal with a problem, or pitch a sale. Many have said they hadn't had a day off in years. They admit that even while on vacation with their families, they took calls, handled contracts, and negotiated sales. Some of them actually said it with pride. When I asked how their family felt about it, they stopped talking.

Unequivocally, a life like that will torture you, kill your marriage, alienate your kids, and lead to burn-out. Assuming it hasn't already. Here is the hard truth: If you want to see your success *and* your family, you need a plan *and* a schedule, and you must create and adhere to a Success Schedule that includes all of the activities in the plan. Can you get to your success without one? Maybe. That is much like jumping into your car in Los Angeles and deciding to drive to New York, with no map, no timeline, no plan. You may get there some day, you may not. But with a destination determined, a plan on how to get there, and a schedule to follow, you will absolutely get there, barring some unforeseen event–and even then, you would likely be able to recalculate, make necessary adjustments, and still get there.

Robbie explained that he just couldn't get out of bed. Again. When he arrived at his office, his assistant was already there, and since he was already behind, he just jumped into the most pressing activity on his desk, and the next thing he knew, the day was over. His daughter had soccer games, and her team was really, really good. He was a dedicated father and husband and supported his family completely. Our call that day started with his realization that he didn't know how he was going to afford to take family to the high school soccer nationals in a few months. He had started the year with a great vision, a great plan, and a great schedule. Three months in, he admitted his financials were a mess, and he was staring down some serious debt. We talked weekly about sticking to the schedule, and repeatedly he found reasons he was unable to do so.

"Robbie, if you keep doing what you have been doing, will you be able to go to nationals with your daughter? Will you even be able to send her?"

"I don't know. No. I don't know."

"What will your life look like at home if your current results continue for another six months?"

"I can't even think about it. The debt I have right now is starting to choke me. I need to quit coaching. I have to cut back everywhere. I may have to let my assistant go. I don't know what else to do."

"But you do. What does your plan say to do?" We reviewed the plan and the Success Statement again. We took a hard look at the schedule he had set for that plan. I asked him to envision that future, six months from now when he had followed the schedule, completed the activities, and achieved the goals. "What does that feel like, Robbie? How does your home life feel now?"

He had before described what his life would look like if things stayed the same, and it was painful. It cut him deeply. Not only for his sake, but for his family he loved so much. And now, as he described what it would be when he achieved his goals, his emotions were stronger, hopeful, resolute. Stepping into the negative future and then into the positive one reignited his passion and connected him once again to the original vision of financial independence.

"So, Robbie, since you've reaffirmed your commitment to your success and your commitment to the plan, let's look at the schedule. What can we change to increase your daily success rate?" Now, with crystal clear understanding about why the schedule was so important, we were able to identify a few issues that plagued his ability to arrive on time and a success habit to ensure consistency in the first four hours of the day. Inspired by his realization of what life would look like if he didn't stick to his plan, Robbie immediately started nailing it. When he saw that sticking to the schedule brought immediate results, he was further motivated to stick to his schedule.

Six months later, Robbie had paid off over $50,000 in debt, gone to nationals with his entire family, and already scheduled a summer vacation. He told me, "I will never be in debt again. That felt so bad; I will never allow that again. For my family's sake, my schedule is my boss." For some, the fear of pain is a stronger motivator than the desire for success. Fine. Whatever it takes.

THE ROUTE: THE SUCCESS SCHEDULE

1. Plan your Perfect Day (figure 1)
   a. Start at the perfect time to get up (e.g., 5:00 a.m. - Wake-up).
   b. In no shorter than 15-minute increments, determine all the key times you must begin a new activity (e.g., arrive at gym, take shower, read a book, arrive at office, repeat affirmations, practice scripts, prospect, lunch, etc., all the way to bedtime). (See sample schedule.)
   c. If you are doing an activity for an hour, no need to break that down; you can label it "10:00 - call database"; and then "11:00 - follow-up calls"; "11:30 - check email," etc.
   d. Include everything that is important to get what you want.
   e. If it isn't on your schedule, you won't do it; you can't do it. So, include things like "5:30 - arrive home" or "have dinner with family." Your loved ones will be happy to see you regularly.

2. Write five Perfect Days, Monday through Friday–your perfect week–and make the necessary modifications according to the things that are important to you, your business, and your family.
   a. If you meet with a networking group on Thursdays at noon, add it. If you have a church group you meet on Wednesday nights, add it. If your children have sporting events or extra-curricular activities you want to attend, include them.
   b. If it isn't in your schedule, you won't do it. Seriously, you CAN'T do it.
   c. If your work week is something other than Monday through Friday, compose your written plan accordingly.

3. Plan your two days off.
   a. If you are starting a new business or a major project, you may not get two days off. That is acceptable for a predetermined amount of time, but that is NOT an acceptable permanent schedule. After a year maximum, you need to

schedule up to two days off per week.

b. If you will do some minor business activity on your day off, create a time-block for it: E.g., "9-10:30 – check emails and return phone calls." For all other time, write DAY OFF

4. Write your Success Schedule on one page (figures 2, 3)
   a. Format the page in two columns.
   b. Even if Monday and Tuesday are exactly the same, write the schedule for both.
   c. Review your plan and make sure everything that needs to be in the schedule to achieve your plan is included. If something is missing, add it. If something is unnecessary, remove it.
   d. Print it and post it on the wall.
   e. Give copies to your team, your spouse, and everyone who is important to you. (Make sure they are in your schedule; otherwise they will be very hurt.)

5. On the year's calendar, block off:
   a. Vacations
   b. Business trips
   c. Education/Seminars
   d. Any other important dates

6. Sign the Success Schedule. You must be absolutely committed to adhering to that schedule, or you are kidding yourself and letting others down.

7. Every night, review the next day's schedule, verify if there is anything that needs to be changed due to the unique needs of that specific day, and make any changes. Then print it and keep it with you all day, each day.

8. Once it has been reviewed and committed to, it cannot be changed, short of an actual emergency.

COMMIT TO COMMIT

This is a biggie. You now have your plan and your schedule. Look it over. Read it over and over. Share it with your spouse. Talk it through. Answer this incredibly important question: *Am I really, really, really committed to following this plan and sticking to this schedule?*

Now, be honest.

Yes? Awesome! Let's go get it done!

No? Awesome! Let's go back, lower the goal, re-create the plan, and time block a new Success Schedule.

Seriously.

I cannot stress enough how important this is. I've never had trouble with commitment. After 35 years of marriage, my wife asked me if I wanted to renew our vows. I responded, "Why? I meant them the first time I said them." Every plan I have written and committed to, I dug in and stuck with it. I had the same schedule for almost ten years. At year seven, the market shifted, and I rearranged my schedule, but it was relatively close to the first one. And then I committed to that, too.

And every client I have had who followed this important step got what they wanted that year. I recently had a woman approach me and say, "I remember you from 20 years ago. You taught a time-block class and said to make sure to block in your family. I did. Best thing I ever did, and I just want to thank you." That was awesome.

I remember the November before my first full year in real estate, I made my plan and wrote my schedule. I realized it was going to be a LOT of work and I would not be home much. With two kids at home, this was going to be hard on my wife. So, I sat down with her, showed her the plan and the schedule, and asked her to commit to it as well. I asked for forgiveness in advance and promised it would be one year only. She agreed.

At the end of that year, I had closed 52 transactions, a little short of my goal of 60. While I concede I didn't spend as much time with my family as I would have liked, the fact is this had already been written into the schedule, eliminating potential misunderstandings and conflict, and this allowed me to build a strong enough foundation over the year that I never had to work that many hours again.

YOU DON'T NEED BALANCE; YOU NEED ALIGNMENT

In Gary Keller's best-selling book *The One Thing*, he said, "Balance is bunk." I knew this already, but he said it better than anyone. You should read that book, by the way. Not because I was on his publishing team at the time of its writing, but because I believe it to be one of the very best business books of all time. Jay Papasan, his writing partner, is literally one of my favorite people on earth, and the time I spent working with the two of them was one of the best seasons in my life.

Anyway, I say it differently, but the idea is similar: *Balance is not a virtue.* I don't think the words "life balance" are found in any testimonies of successful people. No one who accomplished great things, and I mean GREAT THINGS ever stated, "You know, balance is how I got it done." Well, except maybe a tightrope walker.

We don't need balance. We need a goal, a plan, a schedule, and accountability. When we do that right, sometimes we will be out of balance for a while to get what we want, especially at the launch of a new vision. And if we stay accountable, and we adjust the plan and the schedule as needed, we will end up with a schedule that includes our family, time off, healthy habits, and other things that all lead to something that looks a lot like a balanced life.

The point is to NOT focus on balance. Focus on what you really, really, *really* want. You will get the life you always wanted, and I bet it looks somewhat balanced.

THE TOOLBOX

Tool 1: The Perfect Day

I have been writing and implementing the Perfect Day for so long, I cannot remember where it came from. It may be from the Floyd Wickman *Sweathogs* program I took in 1994; or possibly from my former coach Mike Ferry, a real estate guru of the 1990s and early 2000s; or perhaps a book I read years ago. I would love to give credit to someone specifically, as this one thing has made more impact on my life than any other practice. Hands down.

The mechanics of the Perfect Day were discussed earlier, and I want to elaborate a bit more to make sure you are absolutely clear on this. It is that important. When you begin picturing what a perfect day looks like, you must consider everything that is important to you, and the plan that you have made to get you the success you really want. Answer this question: *If I had the most productive day possible, based on the things I value, including the plan I have made for success this year, the things I love to do, and the people I care about, what exactly would that day look like?* And then get as detailed as possible, and include everything that really matters. Here are a few things that cannot be skipped:

- *The time you must wake up and the time you must go to bed.*

These are the bookends. You need enough sleep. I personally have discovered that for me, six hours is enough. I am a bit hyper-active, and I function very well with just six hours. Robbie, in the story before, shared with me that he needed nine hours of sleep. He was actually embarrassed by that, and I had to assure him that no one cared, and if they did, so what? Your schedule isn't about other people, it is about your perfect day, and that starts by getting enough sleep, whatever amount of time that is. When we adjusted his schedule to get the sleep he needed, he showed up to work with the energy he needed to stick to it. It was awesome to see.

- *The time you must begin your work and the time you stop working.*

In order to implement your plan, you need to work on stuff. Remember the strategies and activities we listed? Yeah, someone has to do those things. And you cannot do them for 14 hours a day. Without a schedule, you just might try that. Many people work too many hours in a day and then fail because they are inefficient, unfocused, and ineffective. So, list a specific time you start, and a specific time you stop. The end.

- *Nourishment and rest time*

If you need three square meals a day, as some do, time-block them. If you eat lunch at noon for an hour, so be it. If you only need 30 minutes, that is fine too. Again, it doesn't matter what anyone else thinks; it is YOUR perfect day. If you want an hour, write it down. Pay attention to your energy throughout the day, and make sure you have time blocked to renew it. My schedule for many years as a real estate professional was to prospect for three hours a day. What I found was that three hours straight wore me out. So, after 50 minutes of calling, I would take a ten-minute break. I'd go for a power stroll in the office, looking for other agents who seemed energized, and I'd essentially be an energy vampire, engaging in small talk and drawing energy from them. I know that may seem weird, but it worked for me. Anyway, after a few short, positive interactions, I would head back to my office, put on my headset, and get back to work. Years later, some colleagues who had worked in that office told me that they could set their watch by what time they would see me on my walk-abouts. I take that as a compliment.

- *Any activity that is a key point in time that, if you miss it, affects the rest of the day*

You may have noticed I included "take a shower" on my schedule (figure 1). I remember teaching a class on this and one attendee raised her hand: "Do you really need a reminder to take a shower?" I imagine she was thinking that I possibly had hygiene issues. I don't, by the way.

I explained to the class that in my schedule, if I was in the shower at 6:45 a.m. then I knew that I was on track and the day was good so far. If I hit the shower any time after 6:45, I knew that I needed to pick up the pace in order to arrive in my office at 7:30. Just like the little mile markers on the side of highways in the United States, it is a marker in time to assess where I am in my schedule and whether I am on track or not. If for you, eating breakfast, or getting a cup of coffee in the office break room is a key moment in your day, put a time on it. Remember, this is YOUR perfect day that you get to design so that you are the most effective in the pursuit of what you really want. Extrapolating this one perfect day into the Success Week Schedule follows the same process. You simply need to make sure that everything that is important to you ends up in the schedule. If it isn't blocked in your schedule, then it doesn't exist.

▸ *Chaos time*

In my schedule, for more than ten years selling real estate, I had a time-block I called "Chaos Time." Because of that industry's characteristics of many moving parts, lots of people with various skill levels involved in each transaction, and the reality that I could control only my own behavior, chaos could show up at any time. After a short while of leveraging my schedule, I found chaos to be the biggest pothole of all. So, I decided to schedule chaos. Yep. In Danny T's world, chaos was scheduled from 1 to 2 p.m. daily. A deal was blowing up? I dealt with it at 1 p.m. A client was furious? I was available at 1 p.m.. The world was about to end? It would have to wait until 1 p.m., thank you. My house is on fire? One of my kids needs me? Okay, since my values are God, family, then business, a few things trumped my schedule. But very, very, very few.

When you are creating your schedule, depending on your role, schedule some flex time where you can deal with the unexpected. If you are scheduled to prospect for new business, and you allow current business to keep interrupting you, you will not have any *new* new business. If you don't have new business, you will have no business.

I have had to give this reminder to every client I have ever coached: *Stop putting out fires during your prospecting time. Everything you can do at 9 a.m. can be done at 1 p.m.* Believe it or not, this, too, starts in the mind. You must believe that when you stick to your schedule, you will get what you really want. You must believe that nothing should interrupt your schedule, short of house fire or family needs. When someone demands to speak with you while you are in a time-block, you simply say, "I have an appointment right now; we can talk at 1 p.m." Preferably, if you have an assistant or voicemail, they can say it for you; ideally, you shouldn't be reachable during a time-block unless that time-block is specifically for you to be available.

THE SUCCESS SCHEDULE IS EDITABLE

As you implement the schedule each day, you may notice roadblocks or potholes that seem to constantly slow you down or get you off track. You must assess whether it is an issue with your schedule or with you. Earlier, I mentioned that you need to sign your schedule. I believe this is necessary because when you sign something, you are putting your promise on it. It is a commitment stating that what you have signed is true. Assuming you are a person of integrity, it will bother you when you do not adhere to it, especially considering you gave it to all the people who are important in your path to your success. We will talk much about this in the next chapter, *Accountability*, but for now, let me at least let you know that the schedule can be edited if you determine that it isn't working. This is about you and your success, not about adhering rigidly to some rule or protocol. Once the schedule is edited and you are willing to recommit to it, you may have to reassess the plan and review your Success Vision Statement. Remember, when you wrote the vision, the plan, and the schedule, you only knew what you knew in that moment. Every day, we learn and grow and add to our perspective. It is not abnormal to have to change the schedule or the plan.

However, you shouldn't make changes without careful evaluation. When you put the time into envisioning what success looks like to you, and crafting a plan, the only reason to make changes to the plan is that you find yourself repeatedly unable to accomplish the schedule and/or you are not getting the results you intended (as the story about Robbie above illuminates). In other words, the plan isn't working. This is where a coach can really help. Having someone outside looking in will add to your perspective and help you determine what needs to change.

Tool 2: The Perfect Tomorrow

I created this tool out of necessity. I mentioned in an earlier story that a client named Robbie insisted that it was impossible to have a Success Week Schedule that was repeated each day. Even though I had evidence of many clients, as well as myself, implementing the Success Week tool with impressive results, he simply could not adjust his mindset to accept that as true. Out of desperation, I asked him if he would be willing to create a template schedule for each day, and on the night before, or first thing in the morning, he could edit the schedule based on the specific needs of the upcoming workday, and then agree to stick to it. He agreed that was more doable, and he determined for himself, based on his energy rhythm, that the end of the workday was the appropriate time to employ this tactic. After implementing this tactic, he told me that he'd had the most productive week he had seen in months. He hesitated, and added, "in years."

That is the tool. Set your schedule leveraging the Success Week strategy, creating not a permanent, unchanging calendar, but a template for each day's plan. Depending on what works for you, choose the end of the day before you go home, later before you go to bed, or first thing in the morning before you do any work to review the schedule. Make only the necessary edits based on the specific needs of the day. If you remove something critical to your plan, you must find a place to make it up that day. If you have two hours of prospecting for new business in the schedule, but you absolutely must insert an appointment at that time, you need to find another slot for that prospecting on that same day. The mantra I learned at Keller Williams Realty was, *If you erase, you must replace.*

When you employ this tactic, you will over time build a habit of efficiency. When you monitor your effectiveness each day, you will be able to fine-tune your schedule to improve your timing of the important activities. In time, I am willing to bet that you will find that your weeks end up looking much the same, and yet, you will have the freedom to adjust as necessary. This satisfies the need for freedom, as well as the need for efficiency. Striving for efficiency with your schedule is the only way to get more done with the time you have available for work.

Tool 3: Affirmations

I mentioned earlier that I was introduced to affirmations in the *Sweathogs* program by Floyd Wickman just before I started my first year in real estate. I was still running my construction company during the day and working as a realtor at night and on the weekends. I knew I needed more knowledge to be able to succeed in this new business I intended to start, and someone recommended the *Sweathogs* training program, so I signed up. I adjusted my schedule and decided to believe whatever the trainer said. I learned much about prospecting and growing a real estate business in that program, and, when the idea of affirmations came up, I distinctly remember pushing back on the idea of talking to myself. It sounded dumb. *Crazy people talk to themselves*, I said to myself.

But during the class, I played along, standing up with everyone else and yelling, "I AM A GREAT REALTOR!" The instructor also made us do the "karate chop" chant, where you would act as if you were breaking a block in front of you with your hand, screaming, "Heee-yah!" Picture that. A bunch of grown men and women, in nice suits and dresses, standing uncomfortably in front of our tables, waving our arms and chopping an imaginary block. Totally dumb. I wasn't having it. I came very close to quitting the program.

However, I had made a commitment and paid for the course, and because of how my brain works, I couldn't quit. Because of the way I was raised, I had a belief that turned into a value: once I say I am going to do something, I do it no matter what. While that has gotten me into trouble not a few times, it has also forced me to finish what I started many times when I didn't really feel like it. In this case, it worked out very well. I went from, "I am a great realtor?" (meek and questioning) to "I AM A GREAT REALTOR!" (with energy and conviction). I found myself growing in confidence, knowing that I didn't know everything but that I was capable of learning whatever it was I needed to learn and gaining the skills I needed to be the very best real estate professional in San Antonio, Texas. I went on to rank 32nd in the *Business Journal* in my first year, and by year three, the year I left real estate in October and became a pastor, I ranked as the number nine realtor in the city. I won't say it was all because of affirmations, but the practice of talking to myself each morning had a tremendous impact on my success.

The practice of affirmations is simply you selling yourself a better you.

We discussed earlier in the book the practice of capturing thoughts that are not serving you. Affirmations take that to the next level. Identify any negative thought you have, replace it with a positive affirmation, and speak this new truth to yourself with intention and conviction. Sell yourself on this new truth. You will become what you think about, and the practice of stating affirmations focuses your mind on the very best thoughts. Remember, everything starts in the mind. Your overall success starts in the mind, and your incremental, small victories also start in the mind. Over time, you become the very best you.

So I want you to trust me, as I trusted that instructor years ago. Talk to yourself. Get crazy. Here's how it works:

1. Write out positive statements that reflect the *you* you intend to be. No more than one sheet of paper.
2. Time-block 15 minutes every morning to stand up and repeat the statements with conviction.
3. Each time you find a pothole or roadblock, write an affirmation that counters that issue. Add it to the list and, if you must, remove one affirmation you no longer need. Limit the list to one page.
4. Just before beginning any activity that challenges you, repeat the appropriate affirmation.

Tool 4: Time-Blocking

I have mentioned the phrase "time-blocking" a few times, and I felt we should go a bit deeper into this powerful tool before we move on. This step of Set Your Schedule is time-blocking on steroids. Once you have written your Success Schedule, it is an all-day time-block. It literally blocks out anything that does not belong in your day. It sets boundaries for you that keep you on the road to your success. Have you ever been bowling? Most bowling alleys have the ability to block the gutters so that when the younger kids play, the ball stays on the lane and they are sure to hit the pins every time. Time-blocking does that. When you adhere to your time-block, you will exponentially increase your success rate. You will knock down more pins more often. When you are doing the right thing at the right time, you make yourself an efficiency superhero.

Time-blocking, believe it or not, also starts in the mind. You must agree that your schedule is all-important and cannot be changed. You have to fight the urges to put out fires, solve everyone else's problems, and allow the many potential distractions to pull you from doing what you are scheduled to do at that moment. Even chaos has a time-block.

I challenge you to use the language of time-blocking. When you set an appointment for someone, let them know you have "blocked" that time for them. When you hear ***yourself*** say that word, you are solidifying that you have committed that block of time specifically to them for a specific activity. Nothing will interrupt that time because it is blocked. If it helps, envision walls on both sides of that appointment to deepen the understanding that the appointment is now immovable, and nothing else can enter in. This will enable you to enter into that time with them without distraction and apply focus. Think about it. If you are able to be in each moment with as much focus on the activity of that moment, how effective would you be? And for the person or persons you are working with at that moment, can you see they will be honored to have all of you at that time working on the shared activity?

The habit of time-blocking, and thinking about your day in blocks of time, is the path to efficiency and effectiveness that will propel you towards your success. Your prospecting will be more powerful and gain greater results. Your weekly meetings with your team will be more impactful. Even in the time-blocks you have for those you love, they will experience your full attention and your presence. You will experience life in a more meaningful way as you reduce distractions and practice being present in the activity in each time-block.

Tool 5: My Schedule is My Boss

I alluded to this idea earlier, and it is an affirmation that powered me through the discipline of following my schedule until following my schedule became a habit. I actually titled my schedule "THE BOSS." I posted it on my wall next to my computer screen and referred to it any time I was distracted or uncertain about what I should be doing. I have serious ADD and am very easily distracted. My Boss kept me on track.

Suppose you have a call or an email (during the time-block allowed for calls and emails), and you are asked to meet for a great activity the next day at 9:30. You say, "Let me check with my boss." (You can actually say that, or just say it in your head–your choice.)

You then look at your schedule. If at 9:30, something else is blocked, but the activity they indicate has a time available at 2 p.m., you reply, "I am sorry, but I have an appointment at that time already. I would be happy to meet you at 2." Even when they told you that it was so important to meet at 9:30, more often than not, they will agree to 2 p.m., or whatever time you suggest. If you believe they can only meet you at 9:30, that is in your head. Changing your perfect day doesn't make sense for that particular meeting. If you change your time-block of your perfect day, the day will no longer be perfect. Anchor that belief: *My schedule is the best use of my time; why would I change it because of someone else's needs?* Unless it is your wife or your kids, or someone who ranks higher than your business, the Boss is right. Stick to your schedule.

So, what if it really, really, *really* is a great opportunity and it is worth modifying your schedule? Granted, once in a while, that is actually true. It is rare, but occasionally, you might have to change the schedule at one point in time. I cannot emphasize enough that this should be a rare occasion. If it actually is that great of an opportunity, go ahead and make the change. But here is the deal. If you lose two hours of prospecting time, you must find a place in your schedule that same week to make it up. Your Boss says so. If you have committed to a specific activity for a certain number of hours per week, that does not change. In your daily review of your schedule, you must find a spot in your schedule to make up any lost critical activity. If you do not, you will find yourself behind. It will take longer to get what you really, really, *really* want.

Repeat after me: *My schedule is my boss.*

I can't hear you! Say it again, louder: *My schedule is my boss!*

That, my friends, is the most powerful affirmation you can have, especially if you have a tendency to stray from your time-blocks. The discipline of sticking to it becomes a habit over time. Where you once said, *I'm my own boss and I can do whatever I want,* you will find that *My schedule is my boss!* is actually more freeing, more powerful, and ultimately instrumental in getting what you want.

Tool 6: Just Say No

Another benefit of the schedule is that it empowers you to say no to anything that isn't on it. Let's admit it: when you are on the road to your success, you will come across opportunities. Others will see your success and want to be a part of it or want you to be a part of what they are doing. With your plan in place, and a daily schedule, you have a filter that can very easily answer the question, *Is this opportunity worth my time?* Often, that answer is *no*.

The tool is this: your default answer is *no*. It is much easier to later come back and say you reconsidered, and the answer is now yes than to tell someone you changed your mind, and you cannot do something you committed to. This may feel odd, but I am telling you this has been one key tool that will give you back so much time and power over your schedule. Try this: Someone calls and asks to see you at 10:30 tomorrow morning, and you know you have prospecting scheduled for that particular time. You say, "I'm sorry, I have an appointment at that time, how does 3:30 sound?" Or someone asks to meet you at 5:30, when you know you are having dinner with your family. Same answer. "I'm sorry I have an appointment at that time. I can meet with you tomorrow at 3:30." If your schedule is your boss, and you designed the perfect day and week, then why would you let anyone interrupt that perfect plan? Just say no!

THE POTHOLES

Since executing your schedule is something you must do every day, you will face more potholes and roadblocks than any other step in this formula. In the interest of number of pages, I've reduced this list to the most insidious of potholes. Since there have been many books written about time-blocking and adhering to a schedule, I do suggest that if you find yourself struggling with this step, you should seek out more books on the topic. At the end of this book, I have provided a number of resources I highly recommend, and on my website, you will find an expanded list that I will continue to compile. Every day there is another stack of books on productivity and attaining your goals, and I do my best to read the best of them. You have my email, so if you discover any that have helped you, let me know. While there will never be an end to potholes and roadblocks, we have the capacity to overcome any and all of them because the truth of the matter is that most of them exist only in our minds. Believing that empowers us to find the solution there as well.

1. *I'm a free spirit. A schedule will kill my soul. (D, I)*

I get it. The reason many people end up as entrepreneurs, building and running a business without fear of the unknown, is because they cannot be caged. Their need to be free and flexible is greater than their need for security. This, too, is just an idea you have chosen to believe. Often, I hear my clients protest in some manner similar to this statement, and I must point out that the belief, at its root, is that a schedule is the opposite of freedom. So, let's deal with that.

What do you mean by freedom? Describe that in as much detail as possible. I shared with you earlier about a client who realized what he really wanted was freedom, and I challenged him to describe it to me. He drew a verbal picture of a life where the business ran itself while he was not there, where he could travel when he wanted, go to all of his children's events, play golf a few times a week–looks pretty good to me, too. (However, I really don't like golf, so for me, freedom may be riding my motorcycle all over the country.) I then asked him to describe how he intended to get from his present situation to that freedom he described. He had been in the business for over ten years, and he knew enough to be able to describe a plan that would get him there.

"How long will that take, if you really focus and get very intentional?"

"Five years max," he replied.

"And how long will it take if you do not stick to a schedule?"

Silence.

So, yes, a schedule in some ways is the opposite of being free. But doing whatever you want, whenever you want, is rarely cheap, and definitely not sustainable without passive income or a large trust fund. Building a business that runs without you requires intention and focus and growth. Without a schedule to manage your time, it will take you a much longer time to build that business. The bottom line in this line of thought is, *What do you really, really,* <u>really</u> *want?* Do you want freedom, or do you want *real* freedom? Are you willing to pay the price now to get what you want sooner?

That said, if you require a certain amount of freedom so your soul doesn't die, schedule it. Yes, time-block extra days off, or an early day off to go feed your soul. Your schedule can be anything you want it to be, as long as you are willing to accept the results of that schedule. Let's say you have a need to have three days off a week instead of two. Awesome. Figure out how you can make that work: make a plan, set a schedule, and do that. It may not happen today, but you can aim at it and work to make it happen. Once you are there, if you want to devise a plan to work only three days a week, fantastic. Leverage the tools we have provided in this book: write it out and implement it.

The Success Schedule is your key to acquiring freedom. The perfect day NOW is the perfect day to get you what you want incrementally. Your perfect day down the road may look different. It is a process you must choose to believe in, knowing it will get you what you really want when you stick to it.

2. *Nobody has a perfect day; this is unrealistic. (C, S)*

Okay, I'll give you that one. But remember we talked about the arrow and the target? You need something to aim at if you have any chance whatsoever to hit it. The Success Schedule is the target. When you first start aiming, you may miss the target completely. Just as a typical target has a red center, and the red and white rings move out towards the edge of the target to measure your accuracy, the Success Schedule has a scale. With most of my clients, each week, in their call-prep document I require an assessment of their week. What percentage of their week was spent sticking to the schedule? They must answer, or confess, from 0% (horrible) to 100% (Jesus-like), how do they rate their week? On their best weeks, 70 to 80 percent was a typical answer. Every once in a while, I would see a 90%. I cannot recall a time I saw a spot-on bullseye.

Here is my point: You need the schedule to know what the target is. Every day is practice shooting at that target. *Practice makes excellent* (not perfect, as the saying goes). The goal is a bullseye, but just like the archer who doesn't quit and keeps at it, you keep working to improve your efficiency and effectiveness. Over time, habits are built, and sticking to it at 70% gets easier and easier. Occasionally you have a blow-off day, because you need it. You don't need perfection; you need effort and focus. You need something to aim at. Without a target, you aim at nothing and get what you get. With the Success Schedule as your daily target, you get closer and closer to what you really, really, *really* want.

3. *If my default answer is no, I might lose an opportunity. (Everyone, at first)*

This is true. However, think about the entire process so far. You envisioned what you really wanted, decided how to break that down into what needed to be accomplished this year to be able to have what you really want in five years (or whatever it was for you), created a plan, and set a schedule of the right activities to be done at the right time. Are you with me? It is also true that you devised and designed the schedule only knowing what you knew at the time, and you had no idea what opportunities might crop up along the way. Therefore, it is conceivable that an opportunity of a lifetime will come across your desk, especially if you have become this focused and intentional person whose business is succeeding and growing. People will see it, see you, and want to be in business with you. That happens. Talent attracts talent. I want you to be prepared to have your hero call you up and say, "I have an idea for you." (That happened to me.)

I had my Success Schedule down pat, and my default answer was always no. If I passed on an opportunity, it was because it wasn't specifically in my schedule, and I had no problem whatsoever sticking to the plan. I knew what I wanted, and the clarity I had attained by leveraging the tools I have been sharing in this book made it easy to say no. A few times, when the person I had refused insisted that the opportunity would end at the end of the phone call, I was able to ask them to hold and then set down the phone and think about my options. I could look at my Success Vision Statement, my Success MAP, and my Success Schedule (my boss) and determine if the opportunity was really an opportunity for me at this time, or if it was just another pothole. I say *a few times* because a true opportunity that might be worth changing your schedule and plans for doesn't happen that often. And with that clarity, you are more capable of making a good decision. For me, for those few times, the answer was still no most of the time.

I was sitting at my desk in early January of 2011. The phone rang, and it was Mark Willis, CEO of Keller Williams Realty International at that time. I had met Mark years before, as he recruited me to KW in 2001, when he was the owner of the local office in San Antonio. As he rose up in the ranks, I saw less of him, but he was always amazingly gracious when I crossed his path. In any case, at first I sort of thought the call was a joke, though his voice is distinct, but I eventually figured out it was really him.

"Danny T. How are you, my friend?"

After a few pleasantries, Mark said, "I have an idea for you, and I want you to come up to Austin and meet with me."

I said yes. Fourteen days later, after interviewing with Mary Tennant and Gary Keller, and meeting Jay Papasan, I accepted a position at KWRI and was driving to Austin to start a new role, having no idea where it would ultimately lead me. I was able to say yes and change my life so quickly because part of the Success Vision Statement I had envisioned literally five years earlier was *Work for Gary Keller.* In 2008, after reading the book *Shift,* I wrote down that goal and created a plan to make it happen. I had no idea whether it would work, but it did. It didn't go exactly as I had planned, yet it still worked. I'd said no many times before that day, and because I knew what I wanted and had said no when necessary, I was able to recognize the opportunity I had already envisioned, and I was ready to say yes at the right moment.

When you have a plan mapped out for a journey to a new place, knowing where you are going enables you to go straight or turn when necessary. In the same way, having a clear vision of what you really want and what needs to occur in order to get what you really want empowers you to say yes to the few things that are right, and no to everything else.

4. I keep getting distracted. (I, C and anyone with ADD)

Depending on your preferred behavior, this can be extremely debilitating. Many high performers have some level of Attention Deficit Disorder. That really isn't a joke. I was walking through Zilker park in Austin with my family one weekend and in the middle of a sentence, I said, "Squirrel!" That sounds like an ADD joke, but there was literally a squirrel right by the path, it caught my eye, and something in me required an excited outburst. My girls all looked at me and, in unison, burst out laughing. My oldest daughter, Natalie, who is so much like me that we butt heads occasionally, recognized that I was not joking, and I really was distracted by the squirrel mid-sentence. And she relentlessly mocked me for it. It was a hysterical moment for us all.

Up to this point, we have discussed how important the schedule is, and so you must see that sticking to it, at least at 70%, is critical to your success. Armed with that knowledge, you must then commit to identifying the things that distract you and build your own roadblocks that keep the distractions away from you. If you are distracted in your office by what is going on outside your window, close the blinds. If you are distracted by voices in the other office, wear a headset that covers both ears. If you are distracted by hunger, have energy bars, almonds, or some other, reasonably healthy snack near you at all times. If you are distracted by a trip to the office break room, buy a small refrigerator and keep water or your favorite drink in it in case you get thirsty.

Recognize that being distracted is not a fatal weakness unless you fail to address each distraction as you identify it. A forewarning might be necessary here: don't try to address all distractions all at once. The activity of identifying a distraction and creating a habit response to overcome that distraction is a process worth following. Often, the distraction itself is a habit you need to change. Changing a habit requires energy and intention. If you try to overcome too many at once, your energy level drops, and you may find yourself exhausted. Without the energy resource available, you are likely to fail, or be distracted anyway. So, pick the greatest distraction first, identify the tactic to overcome or block it, and execute. Then, choose another. I'll bring it up again: this is where a coach comes in handy. Your distractions are often seen more clearly by someone on the outside looking in. The good news of all of this is that you can create a schedule that reduces the distractions and increases your efficiency and effectiveness. It is a process requiring awareness and a commitment to excellence.

TEAMIFY

Everyone on your team should have a Success Schedule. Admittedly there are some roles that require less scheduling, and so some flexibility is necessary. That said, I will share that I have my assistants use this scheduling tool to be able to time-block tasks in a manner that creates greater efficiency. Task-switching wastes time, so if your assistant has a variety of tasks, grouping them into blocks can make their day run so much better... they will thank you for it.

I recommend that you have a yearly "Business Planning Retreat" away from the office, perhaps for a morning, possibly a full day if that is something you can orchestrate without a severe interruption of your business. If you have managers or multiple departments, then this meeting should only include your leaders and/or department heads. In this meeting, you must cast the vision for where the company is going and show them how they fit in the vision, as you see it. Your vision for them should be clear but not overly detailed. You need to leave room for them to then envision what it looks like from their perspective and for their role in the company. Once they are bought in, you then must challenge them to take some time to use this exercise to create a Success Vision, MAP and Schedule of their own. Be sure to allow them time to work on that vision, the same day as the retreat, if possible. Either way, make sure there is a deadline so you can confirm everyone is working together and moving towards your yearly, and long-term vision. And don't be cheap... let them do it on company time.

THE POTENTIAL

Imagine with me for a moment: You are sticking to your schedule. You are getting up at the right time each day, and because you went to bed at the right time, you feel rested. You read and engage your mind, work out and engage your body, and arrive right on time for the workday to start. You are fully present for each time-block, whether meeting with someone, prospecting for new business, or completing an important activity of your day. You are effective and efficient, and your day has more than enough time for everything to get done, as it is planned. Even the few things that were not specifically planned and demand your time fall into place because you were prepared for the unknown, the potential chaos. You are ending your day, feeling energized because everything that was intended to be done is done. The people around you are joyful and satisfied. Your business is growing.

You are hitting your daily goals. You are hitting your weekly goals. You are one day closer to your Success Vision. You are having the life you intended, with the ones you intended to experience it with. You lie down to sleep knowing all is well in your world, with the confidence that tomorrow will be another day of success.

How did that feel? If you don't feel a warm fuzzy right now, you didn't do it right. Try it again. This is important to Seeing Success. Since everything starts in our mind, we need to allow our mind to go into the future we desire and imagine the experience we want. You will get what you think about, so you need to be intentional about your thoughts. Seeing Success in your life starts with seeing success every day. See it in your mind, and you will see it in your day. You can have what you really want in your life, and it starts by having what you want each day. Success is not immediate; it is incremental. You cannot be transported to your success, as in the Star Trek transporter that sends people to any destination in an instant. It is a journey that takes time, and the more intentional you are with your time, the more distance towards your success you will travel, each day, day by day.

If you refuse to grow in your imagination, you won't grow in real life.

Ultimately, as you implement the Success Schedule, you will find that you have more freedom, and more time for the things and people you value. When your workday has very few distractions, more efficiency, and more effectiveness, you end up with more time for the things you love and the people you love. You are able to take your days off and go on vacation regularly, and have the life you really, really, *really* want.

4. ACCOUNTABILITY: *Identify Metrics and Track Your Success Journey*

Being accountable is not really a step as much as it is a commitment to integrity and honesty with yourself. I hesitate to call it a lifestyle, but that might not be too far from the definition of accountability. And, frankly, it really isn't hard to do, unless you think it is. But to be clear, without regular and systematic accountability along the way to your success, drift happens. And as in any journey, if you drift long enough, you will find yourself lost.

When using your GPS, whether going cross-country or cross-town, the software checks your position moment by moment, holding you accountable. You entered the destination (Goal - Success Vision), you selected the preferred route (Plan - Success MAP) and you put the car into drive, and you are on your way, following the directions (Success Schedule). The Accountability starts now. The minute you drift off course, miss a turn, or take a detour, the computer recalculates. It shows you immediately that you are off course, and you need to adjust the original plan. It gives you feedback about your progress. It is holding you accountable to the plan to arrive at your intended destination. Still, since you are in the driver's seat, you can choose to listen to the redirects, change your destination, or turn off the GPS and pull over and take a nap. Leveraging your GPS is not surrendering your power of choice. The computer is not an autopilot (at least not at the time of the writing of this book) and you are not giving up your autonomy. It is simply providing highly informed guidance and feedback. It isn't that the computer has even been to that destination before, but that it has much more data than you do, and so it is able to provide explicit guidance. In the same way, being accountable is not giving up control; it is being willing to allow someone in your life who has a different perspective to help you see where you are and how you are doing on your route to your success. You can also use systems and metrics and hold yourself accountable if you have enough discipline, or can't yet afford a coach. The process of accountability brings clarity to the moment. If you are on track, awesome–keep on keeping on. If you have drifted, recalculate.

DRIFT HAPPENS

Think about it. You have a vision of what success looks like to you, you have created a plan and broken that down into strategies and activities that must be completed according to a very specific schedule. Sticking to a schedule day by day at some point will get monotonous. Usually about day two, if you are a D. Depending on your preferred behavior, you will start putting off some of the boring stuff. You will find excellent reasons to avoid some of the activities that you know must be done. I've seen it happen time and again, and I have heard many good reasons why. I've done it, too. I am as good as any other at coming up with excuses–maybe even better. It's the drift. It happens slowly, a little here, a little there, and if you aren't being held accountable regularly, you end up way off course. When you allow your mind to drift too long, you can start second-guessing yourself, doubting the schedule and the plan you worked so hard on crafting. You may tell yourself you aren't enough, you can't do it, and ask, *Who are you, anyway, to want such a big life?* If we are honest with ourselves right now, we must admit that we all have those voices in our head that, at times of weakness, can take us into dark places. However, if we are accountable to someone, and they ask us good questions about our current status in our plan, we can identify the drift earlier and do something about it sooner. That activity of accountability means we must admit to someone that we drifted, maybe because of weakness or even selfishness, and that is not fun. Facing our struggles and weaknesses feels bad. Having to admit to someone that we have failed sucks.

EMBRACE THE SUCK

This phrase comes from the men and women in the military who protect our freedom daily. Those who serve in the U.S. armed forces fall under a highly structured accountability plan with many rules and regulations that must be followed. In some cases, someone dies if they drift too far–literally. Many of the strategies and activities they implement daily are monotonous and repetitive, and some are dangerous. Some just downright suck. A mantra you will hear, if you are fortunate to be in the midst of those heroes, is "Embrace the suck." They are telling themselves, and anyone who needs to hear it, *This needs to be done, and we are the ones to do it, so let's get to it.* That is the perfect picture of accountability. If your Success Vision is truly that important to you, then being regularly accountable is critical to your Success Journey.

It requires honesty and courage to share your Success Vision, your plan, and your schedule with another person, and to report accurately on how you are measuring up to that plan. You have to be vulnerable and admit you don't know everything and that your perspective is limited. When you envision what success looks like to you and utilize the tools in this book that encourages you to think big, double-it, and dig deep to discover what you really, really, *really* want, then sooner or later on your Success Journey, you will find yourself in unfamiliar territory, or even off track. Probably sooner. And that is normal and not at all something to be afraid of. With accountability, you may discover you have been drifting, or possibly headed the wrong way. Remember, you have never been here before, so how in the world could you know everything? But here is something you must believe: failure isn't being off track or drifting; it is being unwilling to face your current situation and deal with it. When you choose not to be accountable and embrace the suck, you risk getting lost on your journey to success. You won't make it, or at the very least, you are taking the extra-long way. Getting what you really want doesn't happen without some form of intentional accountability and purposeful engagement.

YOU ARE HERE

Have you ever been to a large shopping mall, and gotten turned around? I have an amazing sense of direction and have found my way around roadways in cities all over the world, but put me in a mall, and I get lost in just a few minutes. Added to that, I hate to shop. If I must go to a mall, I immediately look for the map, which is always located somewhere near major entries or intersections of large corridors. On that map, you will always find a red dot stating *You are here*, which gives your exact location so you can figure out where everything else is, and where you need to go next. I use a "You are here" form with all of my clients I playfully named, YMWD, pronounced, Yee-MO-wed-dee, as in year, month, week, day. That tracking sheet is much like that map. This is a one-page document designed to keep you accountable to the most important metrics and factors of your overall goals.

Most of us would say that being accountable is good and normal and profitable. At least in public. As true as that is, I have known many "successful" business owners and leaders who, at one time or another, chose to cancel coaching and avoid accountability meetings. They have asserted uncreative reasons why they just don't need a coach or have time for "those meetings." It is not uncommon for top performers to end up pushing others away, especially after repeated success in their careers. They start to believe their own press. They have come to believe a story that they are superstars, and they are fine without that accountability and don't need the help. Sometimes it is rooted in arrogance, but it is really ignorance. When pressed, they are often resistant to fully explaining their reasoning. Most often, they really don't even know why they believe what they believe, and why they are avoiding the assistance that would ensure their continued success. The end of this story is that they eventually find themselves way off course and all alone. Sooner or later, they look around and find themselves lost.

TIME FOR A REST STOP

Another hard truth: Sometimes we do things and just cannot explain why we chose to do so. There is a scene in the movie *Mickey Blue-Eyes* where the character played by actor James Caan asks his apparently mentally challenged son, after he did something ridiculous, "What is wrong with you?"

Several times in the movie the son is asked this question, and always the response is, "I don't know!?" The puzzled look on his face is comical. It is very funny in the movie; but in real life, not so much.

When you hear yourself say, *I don't know*, it is time to pull over into a rest stop and take some time to figure out what and why you don't know. Continuing as if everything is fine is not okay. You need to get alone, or with your accountability partner, and examine everything. It's like pulling over to check your oil, coolant, and air pressure in the tires. If something is wrong, and you keep going, it could be disastrous.

When you are choosing to act, and you have no idea why, that is a red flashing light on your dashboard. In reality, it isn't that you don't know, but that there is something inside your mind you are choosing not to examine. You are likely choosing to *not* think about the reason behind your actions, either because you are afraid of what you will discover, or because you know you are acting selfishly, or arrogantly, and in the moment, you just don't want anyone else's advice. It is sort of like choosing not to look at the navigation screen in your vehicle because you don't want to admit you are off course. I know that sounds ridiculous, but admit it: there are times when you feel like an imposter in your own story, and it is easier to hide. Somehow you believe it is easier to ignore your current situation than to admit you need help. That is fear taking a front seat. But to get what you really want, you need to be the hero of your story, and so courage is a prerequisite. Being accountable requires courage.

When you are on a journey, whether a road trip or your journey to your success, lack of clarity is dangerous. I recall driving to Florida from Texas one time with my family. It was early in the morning before the sun came up, and the fog was so thick I could not even see the road. The traffic was non-existent, and I later realized that was because sensible drivers had pulled over to wait for the fog to lift. Yeah. I had a schedule to keep, and I wasn't having it. Pulling over was not part of my plan. So, I painstakingly inched along, literally unable to see more than a few feet in front of the headlights. Suddenly, from out of the thick behind me appeared an 18-wheeler, much like a scene from a Steven King movie. He passed me at a speed more typical of what you'd see on a bright, sunny day with no traffic. I had a decision to make in that moment, and so I punched it and began drafting behind him. Drafting is when you get your vehicle into the area behind the vehicle in front of you so close that there is no wind. I'm following him from about ten feet from his bumper, going over 60 miles an hour, my knuckles white from the power-grip I have on the steering wheel. The only thing I could see was the back door of his trailer. Despite the fact that I was afraid, I chose to overcome that fear and stay close to the leader who clearly had more perspective than I. In some sense, I borrowed his courage. When the fog finally lifted, we were back on track, and my hands were sore. I realize now that if that driver had actually been insane, rather than what I imagined him to be–a courageous, professional driver who had been up and down this highway so many times he literally had it memorized–I might not be here to write this story.

CLEAR THE FOG

Why that story now? I was in a fog, essentially lost and feeling my way. Someone with more skill and more insight came along and offered to share with me his clarity. Trusting his guidance, I was able to get back on track. In this case, better than back on track; I actually got to my destination ahead of schedule. It is a rough analogy, but accountability is much like that. All of us, in some way or another at some time or another, encounter fog in our journey to our success. It is human nature, and it is normal. It is powerful to admit that we sometimes just don't know what to do next, or we don't know why we are not getting the results we were expecting, and we need help. To not know the answer is not failure. But to not get guidance from someone who has traveled where we are going is just plain dumb.

THE ROUTE: INTENTIONAL ACCOUNTABILITY

1. Create an accountability tracking sheet that you will use to track your year, month, week, and daily (YMWD) goals (one page, a few examples are provided online).
    a. Identify all the required metrics in your plan.
    b. Select the four most critical metrics.
    c. Break them down into monthly, weekly, even daily goals in alignment with your Success Schedule.
    d. Include rating yourself from 1 to 10 on how well you followed your schedule.
    e. Allow room on the sheet for comments
        i. Results of last week's commitments
        ii. Challenges of this past week
        iii. What I commit to do by next week's meeting
2. Partner with a person to meet/call weekly to review the tracking sheet.
    a. Choose a time and day each week and block it solid.
    b. Time-block 15 minutes before the accountability meeting to prepare the accountability form and review the metrics.
    c. Hold the accountability meeting (call, Zoom, or in person).
    d. By the end of the meeting, write out the next week's goals and action steps.
    e. Time-block 15 minutes after the meeting to plan the implementation of any redirects discovered during the accountability session.

3. Time-block quarterly reviews.
    a. Review your Success Plan and performance.
        i. Review your profit and loss statement.
        ii. Review the tracking sheet and add any important metrics.
    b. If you are falling short of quarterly goals:
        i. Adjust activities and schedule and recommit, or
        ii. Adjust goals.
    c. If you are meeting or surpassing your metrics:
        i. Look at yearly goals and determine if you need to increase any of them.
        ii. Adjust activities and schedule, and recommit.

THE TOOLBOX

Tool 1: The Tracking Sheet: YMWD (figures 4-7)

The tracking sheet has three sections: the yearly goals stated clearly, the monthly goals broken down based on the yearly goals, and then a section for weeks, usually broken down into four subsections. Within the weekly section, there is a space for daily goals, if you are in a business that requires daily sales or appointments. (In insurance sales, we need two policies a day) A template is provided in figures 3 & 4 and online for you as a starting place, but be certain to modify it according to the specifics you must attend to weekly. If you have a three-hour time-block for prospecting, but you struggle with keeping it, add a line, "Number of hours of prospecting: ____." The tool is for you and can be modified and crafted to help you focus on the metrics and issues that relate directly with your success. We are all different and face different issues at different times. In my coaching, I appropriately modify the YMWD for each person. And it is okay and normal to have to adjust this page periodically as things change in your Success Journey.

Once you've identified the top four metrics, add the yearly goals of those metrics across the top. This is to always keep them in front of you (besides the documents you should have hanging on your walls in your office, home, and anywhere else you have placed these reminders). Below that, create a table where you have a section for each of the four metrics, with a column for *goal*, *actual*, and *percentage* horizontally. Vertically, you will have a row for *last week*, *this month*, and *this year*. As shown in the example provided, that gives you nine boxes per metric. At a quick glance, once filled out, you will be able to see how well you did this week, where you are in the month, and how far you have gotten for the year. With this level of scrutiny, you will see drift immediately after it occurs.

Below that, I recommend adding "Sticking to my schedule rating: ____" so you can grade your performance each week. Next to that can be "My mindset rating: ____." Since everything starts in the mind, I include this with all of my clients. It is powerful to keep a close eye on your mindset, your attitude, your energy level, or anything else you have noticed that needs your attention. For my coaching style, having that rating listed each week gives me a heads up if something is happening in my client's mind that needs our attention. If the metrics section conveys that the client is behind on their goal, and I can see their opinion of their schedule and mindset performance, it can help identify whether the issue is in the mind, or in the plan. That is not to say my clients, or any of us for that matter, have a crystal-clear picture of our mindset and schedule stick-to-itiveness, but we each have a perspective of how we are doing. A candid conversation will lead to an uncovering of where the issue is. Once you know the real issue, you can do something to correct it. The power of this tool is not the tool, but the conversation about what the tool conveys.

Next, add any additional weekly metrics that might be major indicators of how well you are sticking to the plan. Suppose you are to make 20 contacts a day, and therefore 100 a week. If you enter 80 in that box, and yet you are hitting your number of appointments goal, the tool may be revealing that you are improving your closing skills. Don't make this too complicated, but a few extra metrics, three at most, can help you stay focused on what is really important. Choose them carefully; use them for a while and assess whether they really help. Again, this document can be modified over time as you improve and grow.

After that, include any financial metrics, if they are not already a part of anything above. You can have gross income, net income, or expenses (business and/or personal). Again, as in all of this document, include only the items that mean something to you. The tool is to keep you focused on what is important to you and your success. The greatest key to staying motivated is keeping your eyes on the target, the Success Vision.

There should be about half a page left, and this is for the comments section, as listed above. Include no more than three comment boxes. Following the format I have suggested, you would fill out the first two prior to the accountability meeting and complete the third box at the end of that meeting, or in the fifteen-minute review you have scheduled for after the meeting. I have included a few versions in the appendix and have more online at Iammorecoaching.com.

Done well, the YMWD tracking sheet will create an opportunity for powerful accountability meetings, whether with a professional coach, a peer, or your spouse. Similar to taking a glance at the navigation screen in your vehicle as you drive down the road, taking the time each week to fill it out completely will keep your focus on the things that are important in your business, and identify whether you are on track each week. Like the mall map I mentioned earlier, it says *You are here*. When you check your performance every week, you will see drift as soon as it happens and be able to "recalculate" sooner. Therefore, less time and effort are wasted, and you will have what you really want sooner.

Tool 2: Profit and Loss Statement

I am going to make this very easy: if you do not know what a Profit and Loss Statement (P&L) is, talk to your bookkeeper and have them prepare this for you monthly. You are a business owner, or a professional manager, and you must always be aware of your financial status. This is the financial *You are here*. If you are not doing the monthly books, hire someone immediately. It costs very little, and it will save you so much. When you watch the income and expenses of your business monthly, again, you will see sooner if something is off track. Not only does this help you make adjustments sooner, but you may also even identify a market or business trend (good or bad). And that will help you make the necessary adjustments to face that trend, or even take advantage of it. On your Success Journey, when you see the GPS displaying a turn in the road coming up, you will know if you need to slow down. If you see a straightaway, punch it and hold on tight.

The P&L will list your income and expenses in the important categories of your business, called the *chart of accounts*. The first time you prepare this, or better yet, have your bookkeeper prepare it for you, look at where your money is coming from. If you have multiple income streams in your business, be sure to break that down. For a real estate professional, breaking that down to listings sold and buyers sold may help you identify your strengths, and over time, it will also show your trends. No matter what your business is, over time you can check its health by watching the monthly flow of your income streams. As for the expenses, make sure every critical metric is part of your chart of accounts so you can watch if any expense gets out of whack. If you have any expenses that are paid yearly (usually for a discount, and only if the total expense exceeds $1,000), such as telephone systems or other technology, have your bookkeeper amortize it monthly so you can really see the impact on your business, not just your checking account. In other words, the P&L is not just a general ledger telling you your bank balance. It is an EKG of your income and expenses to determine if the business is healthy. I have included a sample P&L (figure 8) and online at IamMoreCoaching.com.

When I take on a new client, getting their P&L is one of the first things I do. I will go ahead and tattle on them: the vast majority of them did not look at their P&L monthly, if they even had one at all. This isn't to say they lacked intelligence or business acumen, but simply to let you know you are not alone, if you do not currently leverage a P&L. Many entrepreneurs just jump in and go. They feel their way. I admit that is my natural go-to strategy every time I start a new business. I know better now. Leverage the tools, leverage the people who know things you don't, and regularly slow down long enough to find out where you are. From a financial perspective, your P&L will help you tremendously.

Tool 3: The Accountability Meeting

It is crucial to set the format of your accountability meeting to maximize the time spent with your coach, your peer, or whoever you are working with to stay alert and keep an eye on your performance. If you were working with me as your coach, I would have a very specific format, depending on your preferred behavior. Referring to the DISC profiles, for a D personality, my meetings are typically 30 minutes, very direct and structured. The High I would typically be 45 minutes and have a little more time for stories, whether I let them talk a little more than the D, or I share a story to illuminate the core point of that particular call. The High S and High C are also 45 minutes and very structured, but less intense than the D. Typically, the S and C dominants need a little more time to process the specifics. This is not good or bad, just different. I simply recognize we are all different, and having a one-size-fits-all approach doesn't work.

What is your preferred behavior? Awareness is powerful, and crafting your time based on your preferred behavior will strengthen the effectiveness of this meeting. If you like, choose a time-block of 30 to 45 minutes, block the 15 minutes on either side of that block, and anchor it permanently in your schedule. It should be an immovable time for both parties. If you are coaching with a peer, and you are holding each other accountable, then go ahead and block an hour and half to give each of you time to be the focus of the conversation. However you structure it, the purpose of this time is to gain perspective of what you have done, what you are doing, and the results you are getting so you can determine whether you need to make any adjustments. Structure the appointment enough that you do not drift into side topics. When you drift, this meeting can turn into a bitching-fest, storytelling, or a philosophical discussion, none of which are helpful to anyone. This is why I personally believe hiring a professional coach, as soon as you can afford one, is worth every penny. It is their job to keep you focused. And we usually have another call after yours, so we have to stay on time.

Open the call or meeting with the YMWD, or your *You are here* document. Review the primary metrics quickly, and confirm that the previous week's commitments were completed. I require my clients to send me the prep documents either the night before or by 8 a.m. the morning of their coaching day so I have time to review it and look for potential potholes that we may need to discuss. I review that document thoroughly so we don't need to waste precious time on what can be conveyed on paper.

That said, sometimes having to say things out loud to someone can cause you to see something you have overlooked. It is a human dynamic that hearing something spoken, even if we have read it thoroughly, can cause us to process it more fully. Many times, even after having thought about something over and over, it was only when sharing it out loud with someone that I would hear myself say it and suddenly have an epiphany. Talking regularly with someone you respect will do that for you. It illuminates things in a way that deepens your perspective and may cause you to think about an idea in a different way than you had before. Remember, you haven't gone down this road before. If you see something you have never seen, by yourself, you will rely on only what you know. That is how the mind works. But, with a fellow traveler, the potential for learning and growing is magnified.

Once you are clear about where you are, where the conversation will go depends on how you performed the week before. If you are hitting all your weekly goals, and the results are what you expected, you celebrate and anchor that feeling and tie it to the long-term goal. Identify what's next, and look for potential potholes and growth opportunities. That is a fun call.

If you are hitting your weekly goals but are not getting the results you expected, there may be an issue with the original plan, or there may be a skill deficiency. For instance, if you made all the contacts you intended but didn't get the appointments you expected, it could be a skillset issue.

If you are skipping some of the activities, it could be a mindset issue. Drill down, ask questions, and be open to possibility. If you didn't hit your weekly goals, that is what the conversation is about. To be clear, if you don't hit your weekly goals, how can you expect to hit your year-end goals? Deal with this situation immediately. This is drift, and if you drift too long, as we said before, you will be lost.

If you just didn't do what you said you were going to do, and that has happened several weeks in a row, then that is a very different call as well. I have had clients over the years who implemented the Seeing Success formula, and then week after week, simply didn't do the work. As one of my coaches would say, "Their video didn't match their audio." What this tells me is that you really skipped a critical step in the process: *Committing to commit*. If you aren't committed to your schedule, that means you aren't committed to your plan, which means that you aren't really committed to your goal. Yes, sometimes we have a bad week; that does happen. But you can't have four bad weeks in a row. If you do, the truth may be that you are not really committed, and you need to go back to step one. I have had one or two clients over the years who wouldn't deal with that truth, and so I canceled their coaching. Blessed subtractions.

As the call (or meeting) nears the end, you must determine your action steps for the next week. Based on the focus of the call, what specific activities and goals, or adjustments to the plan, will you commit to completing in the upcoming week? Some coaches call this *homework* but what you call it is irrelevant. You must make a commitment to your schedule and the plan and any adjustments each week, and put the commitment in writing. And then you print that document, always keeping it with you during the week and making notations on that sheet to prep for the next week's call.

It aint real till it's written–and it aint really real until you share it with someone who will hold you accountable.

To be crystal clear: this tracker document has your yearly, monthly, weekly, and daily goals clearly written; you update your actual stats each week; calculate any gaps; and update your goals each week so you know exactly what your intentions are for each day and week. You keep it with you at all times; it is like having your GPS on your phone everywhere you go. You absolutely know at every moment where you are and what you need to do to get to where you intend to go.

The intention of the call, regardless of the prior week's performance and results, is to focus–or regain focus and clarity–and set the upcoming week's action plan. It's getting out of your vehicle and cleaning the windshield and checking the tires. It's double-checking the map and making sure you are heading the right way. This must be done, and it must be done weekly. I have been part of a coaching program that had bi-weekly calls as an option, and if that is all you can do for whatever reason, it is better than nothing. But if you want to get what you really want, the accountability meeting should occur every week, rain or shine. The only acceptable reasons for missing are vacation, big holidays, or family emergencies. The accountability meeting is *that* critical to your success.

The professional coach spends years crafting their calls and learning how to assist their clients to self-discover the potholes and roadblocks and gain clarity. There are many books devoted to the accountability conversation, and I leave that to other authors for now. The bottom line for this specific tool is that it must happen weekly, it must have structure, it must begin with identifying where you are at that moment, and it must end with a commitment to do whatever it takes to get back on track, stay focused, and follow the schedule. Remember, you envisioned your success, created a plan, and set a schedule. The focus now is to stick to the schedule. When you do this, week in and week out, you will see your success on the horizon, and eventually, you will have what you really, really, *really* want.

THE POTHOLES

1. *I don't need a coach - I can hold myself accountable. (D, C)*

I understand this one deeply. I have said it to myself, and I said it to my previous coaches in my third year of real estate sales. It isn't that I was deluded, but I was hitting my goals and seriously knocking it out of the park. Mid-way through that year, I had already closed 60 deals, more than I had done my entire first year, which had been a "rookie of the year" performance. I was and still am a highly disciplined person, and I had committed to my schedule so fully that I was crushing it. I was holding myself accountable to a very high standard. Looking back, however, I do see that giving up my coach may have slowed me down just a little. Truthfully, who knows what might have happened had I had that extra insight. While I still ranked number nine realtor by volume closed that year, who is to say I might not have done even better had I kept using a coach? As Ricky Bobby says, "If you ain't first, you're last." But I digress.

I am simply going to ask you to resist this thought. While you may be very disciplined and capable of keeping to your schedule without assistance, having someone who is looking in from the outside will always add perspective, and additional perspective is always better. Seeing more will always provide more information and that information will help you make better decisions. Since this is obvious and you know it is true, if you are resisting having or keeping a coach, something else is going on. You need to slow down a bit and check yourself. Why do you want to reduce your level of accountability? Is it arrogance? Do you now think you are better than everyone around you? If so, I will warn you that arrogance leads to a fall. If you are looking at yourself as better than others, you will end up walking right off a cliff. Arrogance is a success journey killer. You need to recognize that while you may have improved a great deal, you had help along the way. And those around you are growing, too, and capable of so much more than they currently are experiencing. They can grow with you if you humble yourself, or they will grow past you if you separate yourself from them. In short, get over yourself, and keep your coach. Worst case: find a new coach just to shake things up.

2. *I can't afford a coach. (I, S, C)*

This may be true if you have checked your finances and you literally do not have enough money. A good coach, before he or she accepts you into their program, will interview you and look at your current financials. If they find you truly aren't ready financially, they should encourage you to find other ways of being accountable until you increase your income enough to be able to afford one. *Do not go into debt to get a coach.* If you don't have the money yet, follow the Seeing Success process, and in your plan, add *Hire a coach by this date.* Find someone in your life who you can partner with to hold each other accountable until you have reached the financial mark that allows you to pay a professional. It is important that you deal honestly with yourself and do not create a financial situation that ends up putting you into a hole.

Now, if you are saying you cannot afford a coach, and you actually can but you are just being cheap: Stop it! That's a mind-block. You are allowing a limiting belief into your mind, and you need to examine where that thought is coming from. If you really want to get what you really want, look at your Success Vision again, look over your plan, and ask yourself, *Will I get what I want without a high level of accountability?* I'll go ahead and give you the answer: No! That is like jumping into your car to drive across the country and simply choosing to turn off the navigation screen. Yes, you can read the road signs, and you may even be able to find your way. It is possible you will arrive at your destination, but at what cost? It is likely you would have made wrong turns, had to back-track a few times, and hit a traffic jam or two. Professional accountability, like that navigation program, keeps you on track, allows you to adjust quickly, and helps you identify thoughts and actions that are slowing you down. The Seeing Success formula includes accountability because you *will* encounter potholes and roadblocks. A professional coach is the highest form of accountability. Depending on the coach you hire, it could be a fair amount of money. I get it. The question is this, then: *If you aren't willing to invest in yourself, what is the real issue?*

I have had the blessing of traveling the country and teaching thousands of professional salespeople how to get what they want. Whether teaching about mindset or growing their teams and hiring employees, the subject of coaching has almost always come up. It would be comical to point out how many clients at first resisted the idea of paying a person $1000 to $2,000 a month for four 30-minute calls a month. Except it isn't funny at all. Smart and capable men and women have pushed back on this important component of the Seeing Success formula and insisted they could arrive at their success without investing that money. And again, some of them may have found their way. Just way too few.

Mark Willis, former CEO of Keller Williams Realty International, who took the company from 50,000 agents to over 100,000 agents while at the helm, has stated that at various times in his career, he has had numerous coaches for various aspects of his life. He told me he had more than one coach he paid over $75,000 a year. Talk about investing in yourself. Do you know any successful athlete who has no coach? Go ahead: name one. I have read that Tiger Woods, arguably one of the best golfers to ever play the game–and then to not play the game due to surgeries and some rather public personal failures–had up to four coaches at one time. It is not in any way a stretch to say that virtually every person who has seen the success they envisioned for themselves has had some level of accountability to help them stay focused and gain insight into themselves and their plan on their journey to get what they want. More often than not, they had a professional coach.

TEAMIFY

For your team, you may well be the coach of those who report to you, and each of them would be the coach of their team members. Using the appropriate metrics for each department and each role, and also providing training on how to execute the YMWD conversations in a way that provides clarity to all parties, will ensure a cohesiveness to your entire operation. The biggest mistakes companies make is failing to inspect what is going on throughout the company in a thorough manner. Yes, you need to trust your managers and directors and give them some latitude. But without an accountability structure, you will just get what you get, instead of getting what you want.

THE POTENTIAL

You have envisioned your success. You have created your plan, and it is posted on the wall for all to see. You are following your schedule and tracking all of your metrics closely. You are reviewing your performance each week with a partner who asks great questions and helps you to gain clarity about where you are and what you need to adjust to get what you really want. You have your tracking document, and you know your goals and what you need to do next. Your schedule is your boss, and you are sticking to it. You are gaining the skills you need and getting better and better at the key activities of your business. You are seeing successes along the way and learning from the challenges. You are becoming known as a professional, and others in your field recognize you are on a path to greatness. More opportunities are offered to you, and you instantly know whether they are worth seizing or passing by. You have clarity. You have peace. You are energized. You are enjoying the relationships that are important to you. You are growing as a professional and as a person. On your Success Journey to getting what you really, really, *really* want, you are experiencing a life of abundance and joy.

PART III
The Rubber Meets the Road

How are you feeling right now? You have read the four steps to getting what you really, really, *really* want. You have mulled over the information; you have considered the various tools and have maybe even done a little envisioning along the way. You are excited and hopeful, and maybe–just maybe–you are starting to believe you ***can*** pursue that desire deep inside that you have never shared with anyone before. You now see there **is** a path to your big life. It is my hope that you feel inspired and empowered now, and you see that there is a route you can take to get what you want. You not only can, but you should live the abundant life that you deserve and that the universe is designed to give you. You are looking out into the horizon toward your future, and somehow, it is becoming clearer. Hope is growing in your mind, in your spirit, in your heart. THAT is so exciting! You really can have all that you really want!

HOPE IS A HABIT

If you are feeling hopeful right now and preparing yourself to dive into this process, know that you will have to mind your mind. There will be potholes and roadblocks, and you will have to pay close attention to your thought habits. You will need to identify any thoughts that creep in and delay or deter you, thoughts that don't serve you and your success. If you have been more hesitant or negative in the past, those may be habits you developed because you didn't know about the abundance waiting for you. Know this: your past thoughts, habits and inaction do not determine your ultimate success, but that does mean you will have to mind your mind closely, especially at first. You will learn to capture those thoughts that slow you down sooner and develop the new habit of hopefulness. Sure, shit can go very wrong. But it can go very right, too. So, since none of us can tell the future, choose hope and optimism, and get moving.

I feel a need to share this with you: this book is not a part of some plan to become a famous author or gain coaching clients. I don't care about that. I am very satisfied with my life and am enjoying abundance in so many ways. I am having a blast in my abundant life. At the time of this writing, my gorgeous wife and I recently returned from a three-week trip to Italy, and our businesses were run by great people in our absence. We have our dream ranch, with my wife's dream lavender crop growing as we speak. We have no debt. Our kids have wonderful lives, and we just welcomed our third grandchild. We are enjoying what we really want on our way to having what we really want. So…I am good.

IT'S NOT ME – IT'S YOU

This book is not about me; it's about you. I believe that you are supposed to read this, and the universe is just using me right now to tell you to get up and go get what you really, really, *really* want.

I time-blocked an hour a day to put this formula in book form to reach more people than I am currently reaching. I have the opportunity to teach and coach, and I love seeing that *aha!* moment when someone connects the dots and sees a bigger life for themselves. It is exciting to me to hear clients begin to define success for themselves and start creating a plan to get what they really want. It is extraordinarily satisfying to see men and women schedule out their day to increase their effectiveness and efficiency and pursue the abundance that is just waiting for them. This book is just another tool to get the word out. You can have what you really want!

I have taken the time to write this out for you and included stories of others who were in a similar place as you are now, living a *less-than* life. The book is a strategic action I chose to empower more people to get what they want. I have this wild vision of a world where everyone is pursuing the abundant life that they were born to experience. Think about that for a moment: Imagine every person on the planet envisioning a life for themselves that is exciting, big, and in alignment with their passion and purpose, each of them creating a plan, setting a schedule, and taking action. Imagine each person choosing to be accountable to their actions each day, staying humble, grateful, and joyful as they are on their Success Journey. What an amazing world we would live in. And I am crazy enough to think it is actually possible!

My view of this world and of humanity is that every single person is a tiny piece of the reflection of God. Currently, most of us are like those little pieces of shattered mirror, strewn about the world in billions of pieces. And, as each of us begins to pursue the life we are destined for, it is as if the mirror is coming together and reflecting more and more of who God really is. We are created in His image, and we will reflect His image more and more as we pursue the life He has for us: an abundant, joy-filled, purposeful life. God is revealing His majesty in each of us as we grow and become more, as we pursue the life He has intended for us. If that is true, and I believe it without reservation, then we owe it to the world to stop being satisfied with the mediocre *less-than* life, and start living the life we are destined to live. Pursuing a big life is not selfish, or futile. It is holy and sacred. Pursuing abundance is an act of worship and an acknowledgment to God (or the universe or whatever you choose to acknowledge as bigger than you) that you are more than who you are now and that you can have what you really, really, *really* want.

THE ROUTE: *SEEING SUCCESS* IN REAL LIFE

Let's take a quick walk-through of what leveraging this formula in your life might look like. Please note that it isn't a perfect step-by-step that looks the same for everyone, but rather a solid framework by which each of us can navigate from where we are to where we really want to be. It's important that as you read this, you FEEL it. You have to SEE it!

It begins with vision. You begin thinking about what your life might be if the universe fell into alignment and everything went as planned. Your vision starts to become clearer, and what once seemed to be in the far-off horizon starts to take form. You employ the double-It tool and push yourself to think differently, to think bigger. To the best of your current ability, you write down your Success Vision. You read it and it makes your heart race.

With that Success Vision clear in your mind, and having written it down and shared it with those you care about (your spouse, your close friends, your team, your coach or accountability partner), you begin to consider what that would look like in five years. And once that has taken form, then three or two years, until you have a strong sense of what that would look like by the end of this year. Then, you get clear about *Where you are* and the gap between what is now and what is to be. You write out your Success MAP document and share it with those you care about.

You set your Success Schedule and commit to following it each day. You already know some of the mindset potholes you will face, and you write out specific affirmations to help you mind your mind. You envision the perfect day, then the perfect week, and craft your schedule to include everything that is important to you, knowing that if it isn't in your schedule, it won't get done. You write down the schedule, print it out, sign it to commit to it, and share it with those you care about.

You determine the date you will begin and prepare yourself to adjust the way you have done things in the past, to become more intentional about how you live out each day. You want what you want, and you know you can have it, and you know you must follow the schedule and stick to the plan to get it. You remind yourself constantly that abundance is your destiny, and the universe is for you: you will have your success.

As you begin following your schedule, you learn and discover new things daily. You have small successes and face small roadblocks. You hit a few potholes. You celebrate and adjust. You have your accountability meeting and identify what is going as planned and what is not. You celebrate and adjust. You notice the clarity that you have as you follow your Success Schedule each day. You are feeling healthier because your schedule includes exercise, and you are developing healthy habits. Your mind is sharp, and you are learning because you have a time-block for reading each day. You are rested, excited, and hopeful because you are getting the rest you need by following your schedule. You are growing as a professional and as a person and gaining confidence that you will have your success. You are seeing your success more and more clearly as you are becoming more.

You have your first quarterly meeting, and you take a full accounting of where you are in your Success Journey. After reviewing with your accountability partner or coach, you identify a few modifications to your schedule that would increase your effectiveness. You see where you have grown, and you celebrate. You also notice some things you need to improve, and you make adjustments to ensure you gain the knowledge you need to make those improvements. You add a few books to your reading list and schedule a training event to attend. You recommit to the adjusted schedule and press forward.

Six months into your new lifestyle of following a schedule and being accountable, you have new habits that make what once required discipline and effort much more effortless. Your thought habits keep you positive and hopeful. You are healthier and happier, and you are experiencing the life you wanted on your way to the life you really want. Seeing the daily successes adds to your confidence that you will continue to succeed day by day. Others are noticing that something is different about you, and opportunities are being offered to you. You know how to respond because you know what you want. You are saying *no* far more often than you used to, and it feels good!

The time comes to begin planning the next year, and you look back at the past several months to see the successes and the challenges you faced along the way. You are more than you were, and you know deep inside you have more to offer to the world. That thought excites you because you have the confidence to trust yourself and keep moving toward your success. You are confident, not because you know everything, but you know without a doubt that whatever comes your way, you are capable of learning what you need to learn and doing what you need to do to get what you want. You don't know everything you need to know yet, but you know you *can* know. You are becoming more.

You envision your success again and find that your vision has grown. You now know more than you did a year ago, and your vision has become even more clear. You create your plan, write your Success Map, and set your Success Schedule again. You look in the mirror, and you are excited for the future. You are more than you were. You know you will be more tomorrow. And you will have what you really, really, *really* want.

THE TOOLBOX

Tool 1: Get Your Shit Together (GYST)

You may get tired. Get some rest.

You may get bored. Schedule some fun time or take a day off.

You may get distracted. Figure it out and deal with it.

And then, read your Success Vision, and dig deep and find that passion and energy. Read through your Success MAP. Remind yourself of your commitment to the plan. Look at your Success Schedule and get back to doing what you know you need to do. Reach out to your accountability partner and be honest and open about the turmoil you are feeling.

This may seem harsh to some, but let's be real honest: when we drift enough, we can start feeling sorry for ourselves and create a mental environment that is exhausting. While I do understand depression, anxiety, and a lot of the stuff that happens in our minds, I still state that for most people, it is ONLY in our minds. So if that crap is in the mind, that means the solution is also in the mind. Figure out what you need to do to stop being anxious, or depressed, or whatever is in your way. (If your depression or anxiety persists, you should see a physician. Clinical depression is a real thing, and there are drugs and other protocols that can bring healing.) Two things help:

1. Go get involved helping others less fortunate than you. Volunteer at a food bank, work at a soup kitchen, or find an opportunity to give away what you have. Depression is often result of looking inward too much.[10] So look outward to see who you can help, and then get involved and help them. And keep helping them until you understand how good your life is.
2. Revisit your Success Vision. Go to that vision that inspires you; remind yourself why you want it and what it means to you and all the people you love. Dig deep and go there! Go into the future and feel it!
3. If you are dealing with persistent anxiety or something else you aren't sure how to navigate, get help. Read a book. Get counseling if necessary. I will tell you anxiety is often ONLY in the mind, and often you can fix it in your mind. Sometimes you need help; sometimes you need prescription drugs—and that's okay.
4. *If it is to be, it is up to me.* GYST.

10 I acknowledge that depression, bipolar disorder, and other mental illnesses are serious and challenging. I am not referring to this level of illness in this chapter and recognize that seeking professional help is often wise and appropriate.

Tool 2: The Coach

There are many coaches out there. Some real estate offices have coach-ing programs included or in-house. If you search the internet for a coach, you will find thousands of coaches for every type of business. You can try I AM MORE Performance Coaching, but we cannot coach all of you, so please do not call us unless you are dead serious about getting what you really, really, *really* want! We are not the cheap-est, and we won't take everyone. And, as I said, you have many options out there. Figure out what will work best for you, and then do that.

Be sure you have enough money if you hire a coach. You should be able to pay six months in advance; otherwise, do not do it. (Not saying you SHOULD pay them in advance, but that you COULD.) Do not get coaching if you cannot stick to it for a year without adding stress due to finances. And if you don't see marked improvement in six months, get a different coach.

THE POTHOLES

The four steps to the formula look simple on paper. The real-life ap-plication is far messier. I shared with you in each chapter a number of potholes and roadblocks you may encounter on your success journey. It might be good to read back through them and identify those that are specific to you. Again, when you mind your mind and strive for awareness, you are able to identify thought habits that have not served you in the past. Your past does not *define* you, but it does *inform* you. When you take a little time to consider what might get in your way as you pursue your success, your response time will be faster when you do face an obstacle.

The only other pothole we should discuss now is DISTRACTION. It's very easy to get distracted (or is that just me?). We start to see suc-cess and we forget that it was the formula we were following that has brought us this success–so we drift. We start winging it. And next thing you know, we lose momentum and things start falling apart.

That is why a professional coach makes such a difference. If you pay someone $1,000 to $2,000 a month (or more), you are going to pay attention. Even if that coach sucks, you are going to pay attention. If that happens, find another coach, but by all means, mind your mind, have your accountability meetings weekly, and watch for distractions. If you hear yourself making excuses, STOP. Revisit your Success Vision, your MAP, and your Schedule, and recommit.

I'M ALL EARS

I am interested in hearing about your potholes and roadblocks. I have talked to clients for years and worked with them through their struggles as they pursued their Success Vision, so I could write a book just about challenges to success; this book would not have an end if I included them all. So then, know this: You can get what you really, really, *REALLY* want. It isn't easy, but it is worth it. So go get it.

THE POTENTIAL

You are experiencing the life of abundance on your way to the success that you have always wanted. You have no bad debt. You have what you want and are living a generous and relatively stress-free life. You have those you love around you, and they are happy as well.

Now…it's your turn to write out your potential. Whatever that looks like to you, go for it.

LAST WORDS, FOR NOW

I am willing to bet you haven't seen a book quite like this. It's a bit unconventional in style and language. I wrote the way I talk. I wrote what I really think and what I KNOW you need to hear (read).

My hope is that it catches you off-guard and hits you in a way that maybe causes you to think differently. I just want you to read it. And then read it again. And then do it. Use the tools. And go get your big life.

I was talking the other day to one of my employees, and he told me he was talking to a client who used to own an insurance agency for over 20 years. He told my guy, "And I sold that business for over $100,000! And if you work hard you can make over $100,000!"

My employee was nice to him, but unimpressed. He told me that he was thinking, *I plan on making $100,000 in year two, and in five years, make well over $250,000.* And my employee is 23 years old.

How you think is where you go.

Be sure to reach out and email me at CoachDannyT@gmail.com if you have any questions or want to share some thoughts, roadblocks, etc. I would also love to hear your success stories.

Blessings on you and all of yours. Now, get to it.

ACKNOWLEDGMENTS

It is impossible to acknowledge everyone involved in the undertaking of the content leading to this book–as well as this actual book. The truth of the matter is that we all grow every day, and everyone we meet and interact with adds a little of themselves to our makeup. Everything we experience, everything we read, everything we do adds something to the mix which is *us*. If you think about it that way, it is sort of beautiful. We really are all connected. With that in mind I need to thank everyone I have ever met. Dang–that's gonna be a long list.

At the beginning of my training events, I share the concept that what will be happening in that event will be unlike any other event in history, and it can never be repeated exactly. Though I am presenting the same concepts I have shared thousands of times, in that moment, we are uniquely us. Because of that uniqueness, I contend that what can happen is something magical if we all engage, share our ideas, ask our questions, and really dig in. I believe that particular mastermind could produce thoughts that have never been expressed before. Kind of a high bar–but I love a challenge. Based on that, I have to thank everyone who ever attended one of my classes or events, especially if they opened up and engaged. I have seen more breakthroughs and epiphanies than I can count, especially in my mindset classes. I'll cherish those moments forever.

Getting more specific, I want to thank Gary Keller and, by extension, Keller Williams Realty as a whole. I spent eleven years at the brokerage of KW and I definitely drank the Kool-Aid. As an agent,

I learned, and taught all the KW University materials, and I went to over 50 major events to hear Gary speak, as well as hear from all the leaders and extraordinary men and women who were doing big things in the real estate industry. In 2011 Gary hired me and for six years I worked directly for him, and his influence is all over this book. That is when I met my favorite human, Jay Papasan. Technically I was working for Gary, and with Jay, but I learned by listening and watching those two extraordinary men work, and really, just live their lives. Their work ethic, their intelligence, and their commitment to excellence was obvious every day, on every project, and at every level of interaction. I have been influenced in so many ways by them, and I know I am a better person having spent as much time with them as I was able.

I thank all of my coaching clients over the years, whether with MAPS at Keller Williams Realty or with I Am More Coaching. I have learned from each of you and have enjoyed our shared experiences. Just gonna say, *Thanks Robert*!

Several wonderful people from my life at KWRI need to be mentioned, including Mary Tennant, Mark Willis, Mo Anderson, and Jim Talbot, who each taught me much about leadership and navigating through the challenges of growing a large enterprise. From MAPS coaching, Dianna Kokoszka, Ron Patulski and my personal coach, Dru Lee. Their impact on me is immeasurable. My very long-time friend and business partner, Craig Owen, exemplified intentional leadership and to this day still challenges me. I also want to thank my business partner Anthony Azar whose intentionality and attention to detail has made me a better businessperson and leader. I also must mention a newer business partner as well, Shaun Sexton, who is a better, younger me. We are having a lot of fun growing our insurance agency.

I also want to thank my sister, Julie Morgan, and her husband Ronnie, who happens to be my best friend. (I met him first, Julie!) Turns out, Julie is an amazing editor, and she helped me directly with this book in dramatic ways. I learned that the three periods are called ellipses and that you should not use them for *everything*! I also now know what an em dash is...which is fun. Seriously though, if you would have read this book before her many suggestions, corrections, and challenges, you probably wouldn't have liked it. (Assuming you like it now.) I'm just thanking Ronnie because he has been my accountability partner for more than 20 years, and he has influenced my relationship with Jesus more than any one person on the planet. He and Julie are two of the most godly people I know, and it has been fun sharing life with them.

I always tell Jay Papasan he is my favorite human, but the truth is my wife Kat takes that sacred place in my life. She drives me crazy in every way possible, holds me accountable better than any coach in history, and never lets me get away with my shenanigans. And I am a Shenanigator. Just saying. We have spent many mornings, evenings, and drives to the ranch together talking through mindset thoughts and ideas, talking about situations with clients, and selecting wall colors for our many houses we have remodeled over the years. Somehow, this person who knows me better than anyone else still wants me to come home earlier and stay with her as much of each day as possible. It's impossible to express how thankful I am for her.

I could write forever here, so for everyone else I need to thank, I am just going to state this: You know who you are to me because hopefully I have told you in person. I love you and thank you for sharing your heart and mind with me.

Now. Go get what you really, really, REALLY want!

RECOMMENDED BOOKS

Most books take years to write. The author sweats and stresses over every word. Reading is one of the best ways to gain wisdom, knowledge and insight. Reading is rarely a waste of time. The following list are books I have read that have challenged me in the categories I have placed them in (though there are some that defy categorizing):

Mindset:

- Mindset, by Carol Dweck*
- Change Anything, by Kerry Patteron, Joseph Grenny, David Maxfield, Ron McMillan
- The Influencer, by Kerry Patteron, Joseph Grenny,David Maxfield, Ron McMillan and Al Switzler
- Thinking, Fast and Slow, by Daniel Kahneman*
- Give and Take, by Adam Grant
- The Why of Work, by David Ulrich, Webdy Ulrich, Marshall Goldsmith
- A Whole New Mind, by Daniel Pink
- Start With Why, by Simon Sinek
- Mindwise, by Nicholas Epley
- The Motivation Manifesto, by Brendon Burchard*
- Grit, by Eric Greitens

- Inspire, by Patrick King and Kevin Kruse
- The Top Five Regrets of the Dying, by Bronnie Ware
- Awaken the Giant Within, by Tony Robbins (Classic)
- You Can Have What You Want, by Michael Neill*
- The School of Greatness, by Lewis Howes*
- Mindsight, by Daniel Siegel
- Change Your Questions, Change Your Life, by Marilee Adams, and Marshal Goldsmith
- Extreme Ownership, by Jocko Willink and Leif Babin*
- Aspire, by Kevin Hall, Stephen Covey

Time and Productivity:

- The One Thing, by Gary Keller and Jay Papasan *
- The 7 Habits of Highly Effective People, by Franklin Covey*
- The Slight Edge, by Jeff Olson
- Drive, by Daniel Pink
- The Power of Habit, by Charles Duhigg*
- The Innovator's Dilemma, by Clayton Cristensen
- The Lean Startup, by Eric Ries
- Rocket Fuel, by Gino Wickman and Mark C Winters
- Bull's Eye, by Brian Tracy
- Hustle, by Neil Patel, Patrick Vlaskovits ad Jonas Koffler
- Master Your Time Master Your Life, by Brian Tracy*
- Lean In, by Sheryl Sandberg

Sales:

- To Sell is Human, by Daniel Pink
- Little Red Book of Selling , by Jeffrey Gitomer*

Leadership:

- Crucial Conversation, by Kerry Patteron, Joseph Grenny, Ron McMillan and Al Switzler
- Primal Leadership, by Daniel Goleman, Richard Boyatzis and Annie McKee

For Younger people (but I found value as a trainer and presenter):

The Purpose Economy, by Aaron Hurst
The Quarter-Life Breakthrough, by Adam Smiley Poswolsky
Daring Greatly, by Brene Brown*
The Defining Decade, by Meg Jay

Spiritual:

The Life you Always Wanted, by Jon Ortberg **
Everybody, Always by Bob Goff
Love Does by Bob Goff and Donald Miller
The Reason for God, by Timothy Keller
Making Sense of God, by Timothy Keller

* You should read ASAP
** My favorite book of all time

FIGURE 1: PERFECT DAY SAMPLE

PERFECT DAY SAMPLE

- 5:45 AM Wake Up
- 6:00 Go to Gym
- 7:00 Back home
- 7:45 Go to office
- 8:00 Arrive at office - email/facebook
- 8:30 Prep for Lead Gen
- 8:45 Practice Scripts
- 9:00 Lead Gen
- 11:00 Lead Follow Up
- 12:00 Lunch
- 1:00 Appts/Prep for appointments
- 4:30 Home with family
- 6:30 Appts/follow up/off
- 8:30 Home with family/
- 9:30 Read
- 10:00 Lights out

FIGURE 2: SUCCESS SCHEDULE

Success Schedule

MONDAY

5:45 AM	Wake Up
6:00	Go to Gym
7:00	Back home/shower
7:45	Go to office
8:00	Arrive at office - email/Social media
8:30	Prep for Lead Gen
8:45	Practice Scripts
9:00	Lead Gen
11:00	Lead Follow Up
12:00	Lunch
1:00	Appts/Prep for appointments/Chaos
4:30	Home with family
6:30	Appts/follow up/off
8:30	Home with family/
9:30	Read
10:00	Lights out

TUESDAY

5:45 AM	Wake Up
6:00	Go to Gym
7:00	Back home
7:45	Go to office
8:00	Arrive at office - email/ Social media
8:30	Prep for Lead Gen
8:45	Practice Scripts
9:00	Lead Gen
11:00	Lead Follow Up
12:00	Lunch
1:00	Appts/Prep for appointments/Chaos
4:30	Home with family
7:00	Bible/ Home Group
9:00	Home with family/
9:30	Read
10:00	Lights out

WEDNESDAY

5:45 AM	Wake Up
6:00	Go to Gym
7:00	Back home/shower
7:45	Go to office
8:00	Arrive at office - email/ Social media
8:30	Prep for Lead Gen
8:45	Practice Scripts
9:00	Lead Gen
11:00	Lead Follow Up
12:00	Lunch

WED -cont.

1:00	Appts/Prep for appointments/Chaos
4:30	Home with family
6:30	Appts/follow up/off
8:30	Home with family/
9:30	Read
10:00	Lights out

THURSDAY

5:45 AM	Wake Up
6:00	Go to Gym
7:00	Back home
8:00	Church Media Planning
1:00	Office - Chaos - Mop
4:30	Home with family
6:30	Appts/follow up/off
8:30	Home with family/
9:30	Read
10:00	Lights out

FRIDAY

5:45 AM	Wake Up
6:00	Go to Gym
7:00	Back home
7:45	Go to office
8:00	Arrive at office - email/ Social media
8:30	Prep for Lead Gen
8:45	Practice Scripts
9:00	Lead Gen
11:00	Lead Follow Up
12:00	Lunch
1:00	Appts/Prep for appointments/Chaos
4:30	Home with family
6:30	Date Night Kat/Nat/Bex
10:00	Lights out

SATURDAY

9:00	Plan next week
9:30	Absolutely necessary calls
11:00	OFF

SUNDAY

OFF

FIGURE 3: SUCCESS SCHEDULE

Success Schedule

Monday

4:15 Wake
5:00 Walk/Workout/Walk
7:30 Shower
8:00 Search for and Identify Talent
9:00 Leave to Office
9:20 Check Email/Sync with Assistant
10:00 411's
11:00 Discoveries/Present
12:30 Lunch
1:30 KW Leads - compile – email agents
2:00 Discovery/Presentations
6:30 Home

Tuesday

4:15 Wake
5:00 Walk/Workout/Walk
7:30 Shower
8:00 Search for and Identify Talent
9:00 Leave to Office
9:20 Check Email/Sync with Assistant
10:00 KW Leads – email Buyers
11:00 Discoveries/Present
12:30 Lunch
1:30 KW CV visit
3:00 Discovery/Presentations
6:30 Home

Wednesday

4:15 Wake
5:00 Walk/Workout/Walk
7:30 Shower
8:00 Search for and Identify Talent
9:00 Leave to Office
9:20 Check Email/Sync with Assistant
10:00 Discoveries/Present
12:30 Lunch
1:30 RP Visits
3:00 Discovery/Presentations
6:30 Home

Thursday

4:15 Wake
5:00 Walk/Workout/Walk
7:30 Shower
8:00 Search for and Identify Talent
9:00 Leave to Office
9:20 Check Email/Sync with Assistant
10:00 Team Meeting
11:00 Discoveries/Present
12:30 Lunch
1:30 RP Visits
3:00 Discovery/Presentations
6:30 Home

Friday

4:15 Wake
5:00 Walk/Workout/Walk
7:30 Shower
8:00 Search for and Identify Talent
9:00 Leave to Office
9:20 Check Email/Sync with Assistant
10:00 Discoveries/Present
12:30 Lunch
1:30 Discovery/Presentations
5:30 Home

Saturday

If necessary, interviews with Talent

Sunday

Off

FIGURE 4: YMWD SAMPLE - REALTOR

Name:	Date:

Totals	Listing Appts			Listings Taken				Closings			GCI (income)		
	Actual	Goal	% of Goal	Actual	Goal	% of Goal		Actual	Goal	% of Goal	Actual	Goal	% of Goal
Last Week													
MTD													
YTD													

"Stick to my schedule" rating:		Mindset Rating:	

Weekly Contacts				Active Listings	Current Pending Contracts			
Actual:		Goal			This Month:		Total:	

Monthly Personal Expenses	Monthly Business Expenses	Current Profit

Homework from Last Week & Results:

Challenges/Updates or Questions/Focus for this call:

Commitments/Plan of Action for Next Week:

FIGURE 5: YMWD SAMPLE - LOAN ORIGINATOR

Name:	Date:

Totals	App Leads			Apps Taken				Closings			GCI (income)		
	Actual	Goal	% of Goal	Actual	Goal	% of Goal		Actual	Goal	% of Goal	Actual	Goal	% of Goal
Last Week													
MTD													
YTD													

"Stick to my schedule" rating:		Mindset Rating:	

Weekly Contacts				apps with contracts	Current pending final closing			
Actual:		Goal			This Month:		Total:	

Monthly Personal Expenses	Monthly Business Expenses	Current Profit

Homework from Last Week & Results:

Challenges/Updates or Questions/Focus for this call:

Commitments/Plan of Action for Next Week:

FIGURE 6: YMWD TYPE 2 - INSURANCE AGENT

YMWD Accountability Tracking Sheet

4 ©copyright I AM MORE Coaching 2022

THIS YEAR			
Name: Mickey Mouse	Date: 1/1/2023	End of Year Goals	YTD
I want to increase my RP network, increase policy per account, and average 15k monthly premium. By doing this it would generate more money and allow me to start putting back money into my savings to buy assets in the future.	New Business $	180000	
	New RPs	20	
	EOY PIF	485	
	Net Income	75000	

THIS MONTH			
January		End of Month Goals:	MTD
I need to reach out to more potential RPs and ask for business. Make more in person visits. Go to all the events to put my face and name out there	New Business $	10k	
	# of New Binds	32	
	Bonus Goal	9k	
	RP Visits	60	

WEEK 1

Goal		Daily	Actual	EOW Biz $: 4756
Disc	10	2	9	
Qte	15	3	15	
Pres	15	3	14	
Bnd	12	3	10	
RP	15	3	12	

Biggest Challenge:

WEEK 2

Goal		Daily	Actual	EOW Biz $:
Disc	10	2		
Qte	15	3		
Pres	15	3		
Bnd	12	3		
RP	5	3		

Biggest Challenge:

WEEK 3

Goal		Daily	Actual	EOW Biz $:
Disc				
Qte				
Pres				
Bnd				
RP				

Biggest Challenge:

WEEK 4

Goal		Daily	Actual	EOW Biz $:
Disc				
Qte				
Pres				
Bnd				
RP				

Biggest Challenge:

WEEK 5

Goal		Daily	Actual	EOW Biz $:
Disc				
Qte				
Pres				
Bnd				
RP				

FIGURE 7: YMWD TYPE 2 - REALTOR

YMWD Accountability Tracking Sheet - Realtor

THIS YEAR				End of Year Goals		YTD
Name:	Mickey Mouse	Date:	1/1/2023			
Close 48 Transactions				Gross Commish	432000	
Buy new car for wife				Listings taken	40	
Read 12 books				Buyer Sales	24	
				Net Income	200000	

THIS MONTH	End of Month Goals:		MTD
January			
Send out new year letter ASAP	Gross Commish	36000	8325
Call Sphere 3 hours per day	Listings Taken	4	1
4 listings	Buyer Contracts	2	1
4 buyer contracts	Listing Appts	8	2

WEEK 1

Goal		Daily	Actual	Mindset?	8	
L Appts	2	1	2			
B Appts	1	1	1			
L taken	1		1			
Closed	1		1			
GCI	9000		8325			
Biggest Challenge:						

WEEK 2

Goal		Daily	Actual	Mindset?		
L Appts	2	1				
B Appts	1	1				
L Taken	1					
Closed	1					
GCI	9625					
Biggest Challenge:						

WEEK 3

Goal		Daily		Mindset?		
L Appts						
B Appts						
L Taken						
Closed						
GCI			Actual			
Biggest Challenge:						

WEEK 4

Goal		Daily	Actual	Mindset?		
L Appts						
B Appts						
L Taken						
Closed						
GCI						
Biggest Challenge:						

FIGURE 8: SAMPLE PROFIT & LOSS STATEMENT

INSURANCE AGENCY
Profit and Loss
January - June, 2021

	Jun 2021	Total
Income		
Sales		0.00
Total Agency Fees (New)	3,570.00	22,350.00
Total Commissions (New)	17,484.23	153,444.66
Total Commissions (Renewal)	35,527.55	175,661.76
UC Install	300.00	1,200.00
Total Sales	$ 56,881.78	$ 352,656.42
Other Income	$ 670.00	$ 3,980.00
Total Income	$ 57,551.78	$ 356,636.42
Gross Profit	$ 57,551.78	$ 356,636.42
Expenses		
Advertising & Promotion	99.08	3,562.11
Annual fee		1,000.00
Total Advertising & Promotion	$ 99.08	$ 4,562.11
Credit Card Fees	23.92	181.64
E&O Insurance	60.00	1,495.10
Franchise Fees	19,410.12	99,966.81
Insurance	1,475.28	8,897.50
Meals and Entertainment	30.49	74.49
MVR Fees	170.01	1,370.96
Other General and Admin Expenses	778.07	5,211.89
Payroll Taxes and Expenses		0.00
Payroll Fees	125.52	1,019.37
Taxes	1,327.04	9,011.45
Wages	17,346.86	99,859.28
Total Payroll Taxes and Expenses	$ 18,799.42	$ 109,890.10
Professional Fees		372.60
Rent		1,610.00
Software Licenses/Support	1,050.00	6,000.00
Training	(500.00)	6,450.00
Utilities	64.99	325.92
Website	54.95	329.70
Total Expenses	$ 41,516.33	$ 246,738.82
Net Operating Income	$ 16,035.45	$ 109,897.60
Net Income	$ 16,035.45	$ 109,897.60

For these and more downloadable samples and templates, visit www.Iammorecoaching.com

Questions? Email DannyT at coachdannyt@gmail.com

Looking for a coach? Visit www.Iammorecoaching.com and learn more. Applications are available online. Danny and Kat have limited availability and require strict adherence to our interview process.

Made in the USA
Columbia, SC
27 February 2024

e5efac44-ef4b-4ef6-9d34-4654b5185687R02